Alex Ritsema

HELIGOLAND, PAST AND PRESENT

Copyright 2007 by Alex Ritsema

All rights reserved.

No part of this book may be reproduced in any form or by any electronic or mechanical means, including information storage and retrieval systems, without written permission from the publisher, except by a reviewer who may quote passages in a review.

Published by Lulu (www.lulu.com).

Copyright illustrations throughout the book are indicated in each illustration; some illustrations were particularly made for this book, by Anneke de Vries, www.annekedevries.nl.

The front- and backcovers (including text) were designed by Alex Ritsema. The photo on the front cover was made by Alex Ritsema. The two pictures on the backside were supplied by the Heligoland Museum: the upper one shows the island in 1713 and the lower one shows islanders around 1850. The drawing on the title page shows Kittiwakes (*Rissa tridactyla*), drawn by Anneke de Vries, from a photo by Alex Ritsema.

ISBN 978-1-84753-190-2

CONTENTS

PREFACE AND ACKNOWLEDGEMENTS — *5*
CHAPTER 1. Explore Heligoland! — *7*
CHAPTER 2. Landscape, geology and archaeology — *14*
CHAPTER 3. Wildlife — *28*
CHAPTER 4. Legends of saints and pirates (c.700-c.1600) — *39*
CHAPTER 5. Socioeconomic history (until c.1940) — *44*
CHAPTER 6. Heligoland under the Hanse and Schleswig-Gottorp, c.1400-1714 — *54*
CHAPTER 7. Heligoland is Danish (1714-1807) — *62*
CHAPTER 8. Heligoland is British (1807-1890) — *69*
CHAPTER 9. Heligoland is German (since 1890) — *90*
APPENDIX: population statistics — *105*
LITERATURE — *110*

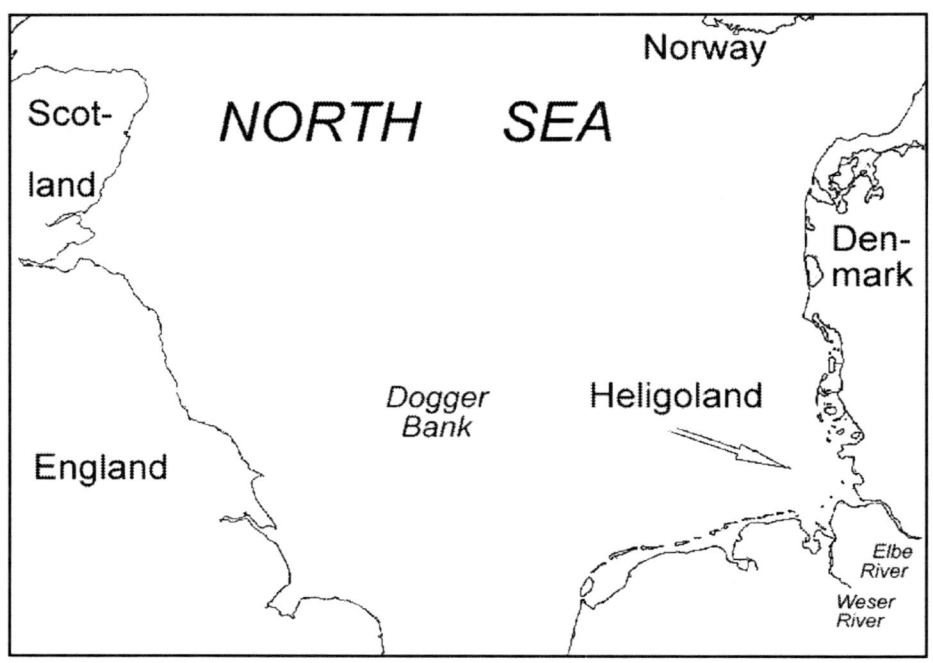

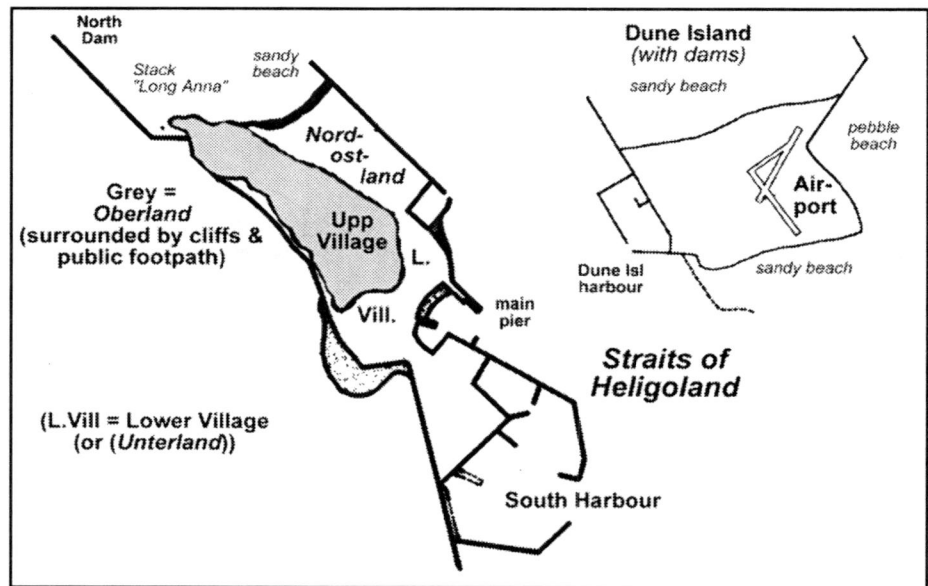

Modern Heligoland (length app. 2,000 meters, excluding the northern dam) (both pictures from Die Küste, *1990, adjusted for English readers).*

PREFACE AND ACKNOWLEDGEMENTS

Small islands have always fascinated me. As a child, growing up in the town of Groningen in the northeast of The Netherlands, I often searched in atlases and so I knew there was a mysterious rocky islet with a length of less than two kilometres, located some 150 kilometres to the northeast of my native town. The rocky island was called *Helgoland*, which is the name in Dutch and German; throughout this book I use the English name with an "i" in it, *Heligoland*.

As a child, I also learnt from a historic atlas that Heligoland had been a British colony during most of the 19th century. I also had – and still take – a great interest in bird life and I discovered that Heligoland was often mentioned in birder's guides because of the many rare bird species visiting the island, especially during spring and autumn migrations.

In the spring of 1989 I made a day-trip to Heligoland with a high-speed-catamaran from Eemshaven, close to Groningen; this connection had never existed before. I walked around the *Klippenrandweg* (literally "cliff edge footpath"), enjoying the red sandstone cliffs and the breeding seabirds on the cliff-edges. In an island bookshop I purchased a book that became one of my favourites: *Die Lustfahrt nach Helgoland* (freely translated "Fun Trips to Heligoland"), an anthology of stories from visitors to the island in former times, especially the 19th century.

Since 1988 all my holidays have been on or near small islands, always exploring them and making a comprehensive slide series. My "small-island-hobby" is not only a *holiday*-hobby but also a hobby at *home*: collecting and reading books, articles, etc. on geology, wildlife and history. My hobby also resulted in my books *Discover the Islands of Ireland* (early 1999) and *A Dutch Castaway on Ascension Island* in 1725 (early 2006) and to my website about my island visits (www.aworldofislands.com).

In May 2005 I went to Heligoland for a holiday of a few days. Among other things, I attended a speech by the island expert on geology, Hans

Stühmer. I started collecting part of the immense literature about Heligoland – almost all written in German, a language that I can read and speak but hardly write. It appeared there was not yet a book in English dealing with the unique geology, biology and military and socioeconomic history of this island and so I decided to prepare this book.

From 2005 to 2007 I visited Heligoland in spring, summer, autumn and winter. Most visitors only make a day-trip in summer – when the islanders, of course, have to make the bulk of their money - but Heligoland has enough to offer in all seasons: numerous bird chicks in spring, migratory birds in spring and autumn, births of Grey Seals on Dune Island around Christmas, to mention but a few!

Many people have directly or indirectly contributed to the creation of this book. I can't mention them all but I would like to thank the following people for their assistance with this book:
- Joerg Andres (Heligoland Museum) for searching illustration material;
- Erich-Nummel Krüss (Heligoland-Museum) for giving important information about the island's socioeconomic history;
- Hans Stühmer (Heligoland) for giving important geological information about the island and critically reading my texts;
- Roel Teeninga for making many excellent scans of pictures;
- Ivo Peeters for helping me translate some German texts (especially eyewitness accounts from former times) into English;
- Marion van Beek for improving style and grammar of the text (as she did with my previous books *Discover the Islands of Ireland* and *A Dutch Castaway on Ascension Island in 1725*);
- Anneke de Vries for making wondeful line drawings (as she did with my previous book *A Dutch Castaway on Ascension Island in 1725*).

Deventer, The Netherlands, February 2007

CHAPTER 1. Explore Heligoland!

In the south-east corner of the North Sea and some 50 kilometres from the German mainland, we find Heligoland, consisting of two tiny islands. The main island – often simply called "Heligoland" - is less than two kilometres long and has red-coloured sandstone cliffs that often rise to some 50 metres. The smaller island, Dune Island, has low sand dunes and lies about one kilometre to the east. Both islands attract thousands of tourists a year.

Some statistics about Heligoland:

- Latitude of the main lighthouse: 54 degrees, 10 minutes, 57 seconds North;
- Longitude of the main lighthouse: 7 degrees, 53 minutes, 01 seconds East of Greenwich;
- Size of the main (rocky) island: app. 80 hectares (maximum length app. 2,000 meters, excluding the northern dam);
- Size of Dune Island: app. 40 hectares (maximum length app. 1,000 metres, excluding dams);
- Highest point (on the rocky island): 61 metres;
- Political status: a community in *Kreis* Pinneberg in the German *Bundesland* Schleswig-Holstein;
- Number of inhabitants (2007): app. 1,400;
- Number of visitor beds (2007): app. 2,500.

The islanders have never been able to live off their tiny amount of land and so they had to live on fishing, wrecking and piloting overseas ships into the nearby mainland harbours as Bremen and Hamburg. Strategically important, the island was often disputed by various great powers. However, the islanders have always stayed "Heligolanders", part of the Frisians. Some islanders still speak *Halunder*, the language of the island.

Nowadays, the major source of income for the islanders is, of course, mass tourism, especially in summer. During high season daytrips can be made from mainland towns like Hamburg, Cuxhaven and Bremerhaven, by traditional ferries, catamarans and small passenger aircraft. Large traditional ferries have to anchor to the south and southeast of the main island and the passengers are disembarked in small boats. If you plan a day-trip by plane you should keep in mind that Heligoland Airport is located on Dune Island!

Some day-trippers are sportive and walk around the whole main island, with the magnificent views from the *Klippenrandweg* – literally "cliff-edge-footpath" – as the highlight of their day. In the breeding season, many seabirds can be seen on the cliff-edges from the *Klippenrandweg*. At the far – northern - end of the island we find a beautiful sandstone stack, the renowned *Lange Anna*. At low tide, one can also see the *Felswatt*, the rocky tidal flat to the west and north.

The north point of the island, with the stack Lange Anna. *Mark the diagonal sandstone laters (by Anneke de Vries, from a photo by the author).*

Heligoland is also popular because the island is a tax haven inside Germany, without VAT or excise duties. As a result, Heligoland has many shops selling spirits, perfume and tobacco!

The main island has five distinctive parts:
- the *Oberland* ("upper land") or the land surrounded by the sandstone cliffs. The south-east corner of the *Oberland* is covered by the island village; the rest is pasture with grazing cattle and sheep. The renowned *Klippenrandweg* encircles the *Oberland*;
- the *Mittelland* ("middle land"), an area resembling a volcanic crater. Formerly this area was the south of the *Oberland* but on 18 April 1947 the area was blown up by British military and so the present *Mittelland* came into being;
- the *Unterland* ("low land"), the low land just to the south of the *Oberland*. The *Unterland* is completely covered by the island village;
- the *Südhafen* ("south harbour"), the artificial land in the south. The original *Südhafen* was built between 1900 and 1916;
- the *Nordostland* ("northeastern land"), an area of artificial low land in the northeast, made by order of the Nazis in the late 1930s. Here we find the swimming pool (with hot seawater throughout the year), the museum, the public aquarium, the youth hostel, sport fields and the – unique and nature-friendly – power plants for heating, electricity and drinking-water.

To explore both islands thoroughly, it is necessary to stay a few nights; simply look (or book) at www.helgoland.de. Interesting things to do:
- visit the museum[1] in the *Nordseehalle* in the *Nordostland*. The museum has excellent exhibitions of the island's history and geology, with many stones, minerals and fossils;
- visit the Aquarium[2] near the northeast harbour with its excellent exhibition of the underwater world of the rocky bottom around Heligoland;

---

[1] website http://www.museum-helgoland.de/

[2] website http://www.awi-bremerhaven.de/BAH/aquarium.html

- make a boat excursion trip around the rocky island;
- make an excursion into the Nazi underground bunkers (inform at the tourist office);
- visit the famous bird catching garden on the *Oberland* (inform at the tourist office)[3];
- swim in the public swimming pool in the *Nordostland*, with hot seawater throughout the year;
- stroll on Dune Island, with its many seals, birds and beaches (see the next paragraph);
- inform at the tourist office about lectures, excursions and cultural activities, such as folk dance demonstrations.

Folk dancers in the Nordseehalle *(by Anneke de Vries, from a photo by the author). The typical Heligoland (under) skirt can be seen from behind; it is scarlet with a broad yellow band on the bottom. In summer there are also demonstrations in the open air.*

---

[3] website http://www.fh-oow.de/cms/ifv/index.php?action=sprache&lang=de

Exploring Dune Island

Dune Island is well worth visiting for swimming, walking and for nature: birds, seals, shells, seaweed, flowers and stones, including flints and fossils. The island has four coasts: the west coast, including the harbour, consists of concrete and basalt blocks, the north and south coasts have sandy beaches and the east coast has a pebble beach, attracting many amateur geologists. Nobody lives permanently on the island but in the tourist season there are two restaurants, one at the airport and one at the south beach. At the airport we also find a small convenience shop. In high season visitors can camp on the camping spot or rent a summerhouse. The interior of Dune Island is lushly green, with interesting and even rare vegetation. The island has footpaths leading to the kindergarten, the camping spot, the airport, the viewpoint-dune, the mini golf course, two fresh water ponds and the *Friedhof der Namenlosen*, the cemetery of the anonymous.

Present Dune Island has a size of about 40 hectares and is, in fact, artificial. In the late 1930s the island was enlarged from a size of only some 5 hectares to its present size for military aspirations of the Nazi rulers. Until 1711 there were even *white* cliffs – consisting of limestone and chalk - just north of the present north shore. Nowadays, at very low tides, the bottom of those cliffs is still visible beyond the north shore.

The south beach of Dune Island (by Anneke de Vries, from photos by the author).

Wi lear Halunder (or We learn Heligolandic)

The Heligoland language (*Halunder*) is a unique "Frisian" language that is still spoken by a few islanders. The language can be learnt in summer courses. Here are a few geographical names in three languages.

Halunder	German	English
deat Lünn[4]	*Helgoland*	Heligoland
de Hallem	*die Düne*	Dune Island
Places and streets in the village		
Wüpp	*Fahrstuhl*	elevator
de Bräii	*die Landungsbrücke*	the landing pier
Lung Wai	*Langer Weg (Strasse)*	Long Way (Road)
bi / langs Strunn	*am (Süd-) Strand*	on the (south) beach
die Berri / Berriger	*die (Helgoländer) Treppe(n)*	the (Heligoland) staircase(s)
Om Wass	*Nach Westen*	To the West
Ool Komeedi Wai	*Alter-Theater-Weg*	Old Theatre Road
Bop Stak	*Hinter dem Zaun*	Behind the fence/fencing
Hingsgars	*Pferdeweide*	Horse Meadow
Cliffs and isolated rocks on the west coast, from south to north		
Di Karkjaar en siin Wüf	*Der Pastor und seine Frau*	The Priest and his Wife[5]
Groot Kark	*Grosse Kirche*	Large Church
Letj Kark	*Kleine Kirche*	Small/Little Church
Seliger Hörn	*Seehundshorn*	Seal Cliff
Skittenhörn	*Lummenfelsen*	Guillemot's Cliffs[6]
Nathurnstack	*(Fels) Lange Anna*	(Stack) Long Anna

---

[4] Literally, *deat Lünn* means "the land".

[5] Two large rocks close to one another at the foot of the cliffs.

[6] "Guillemot" is one of the breeding seabirds of Heligoland (scientific name *Uria aalge*, German *Lumme* or *Trotellumme*.

The famous rhyme about Heligoland

English:
Green is the land
Red is the cliff
White is the sand
Those make the flag of Heligoland!

German:
Grün ist das Land
rot ist die Kant
weiss ist der Sand
Das sind die Farben von Helgoland!

Halunder (Heligoland language):
Green es deat Lünn
road es de Kant
witt es de Sunn
Deät es deät Woapen van't Hillige Lünn!

CHAPTER 2. Landscape, geology and archaeology

The rocks of Heligoland are unique within their vast surroundings. The *Oberland* and *Felswatt* (rocky tidal flat) consist of *sandstone*; when standing on the edge of the cliffs or on board a boat, you don't need to be a geologist to notice the island's many diagonal red sandstone layers, interrupted by a few bright sandstone layers with thicknesses up to some 40 centimetres. The bright layers are called *Katersande* in German and consist of much softer sandstone than the red layers. Until 1711 there was also the *Wittkliff* – white cliffs consisting of limestone and Cretaceous material - just north of present Dune Island; at extremely low tides, some lower parts of those cliffs are still visible. In fact, there is a sea bottom area of some 50 square kilometres around Heligoland with many rocky parts, the so-called *Helgoländer Felssockel* (meaning "Heligoland rocky base", see below).

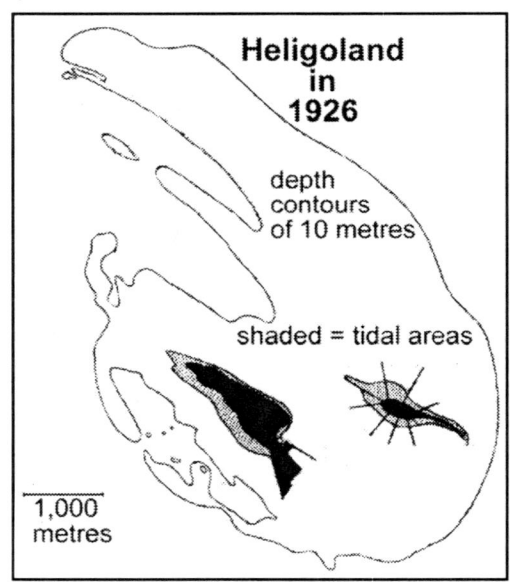

This picture shows the depth lines of 10 metres in 1926 (modern depth lines are hardly different), roughly indicating the area Helgoländer Felssockel. *Deep water (down to 30 metres and more) is found especially to the north, south and west. During the last Ice Age there was almost certainly a land bridge to the east, towards the mainland of modern Holstein (map from Olaf Goemann,* Echt Helgoländer Hummer, *1990, simplified).*

How did this remarkable rock complex come into being? Geologists tell us that sandstone is formed *underground* by compression of deposits over millions of years; so, Heligoland's sandstone was once below the surface! Geologists also tell us that limestone is formed on the bottom of shallow warm seas, as a result of accumulation of billions of deceased creatures. The following question rises; how did the underground stone layers come to the surface in an area without volcanism or earthquakes? To make matters more complex, Heligoland's sandstone layers are lying *diagonally* – at slopes between about 22 and 26 degrees - whereas they were doubtless formed *horizontally*. In short, we need explanations for the following:

- why does Heligoland sandstone have a distinctive red colour?
- why are some red sandstone layers interrupted by bright sandstone layers, the so-called *Katersande*?
- how and when did Heligoland's sandstone and limestone originate?
- how and when did Heligoland emerge?
- why are Heligoland's stone layers – which must have been formed underground in a horizontal position - oriented diagonally?

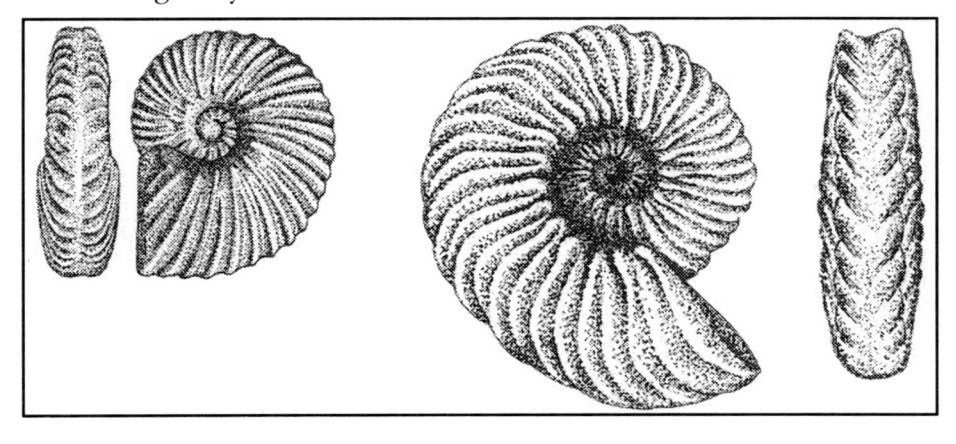

Fossils of ammonites (extinct chalk-containing creatures that were once living on the ocean floor) of Heligoland dating from the Upper Cretaceous; most Heligoland fossils date from that – relatively recent – period. To the left we see Hoplites dentatus *and to the right an example of the genus* Dimorphoplites *(from 'Helgoland, Portrait einer Felseninsel', 1979). The Heligoland Museum has a superb exhibition of stones like these.*

Heligoland's geologic base

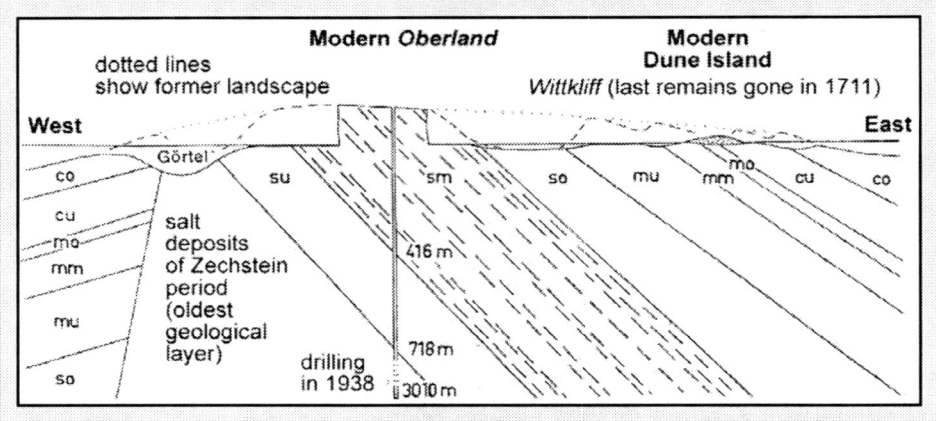

[Figure: Geological cross-section showing layers beneath Heligoland from West to East. Labels include "Modern Oberland", "dotted lines show former landscape", "Modern Dune Island", "Wittkliff (last remains gone in 1711)", "Görtel", "salt deposits of Zechstein period (oldest geological layer)", "drilling in 1938", with depths 416 m, 718 m, 3010 m. Layer abbreviations: co, su, cu, mo, mm, mu, so, sm, so, mu, mm, cu, co.]

Geological layers in and around Heligoland. The horizontal line shows the modern sea level. All layers were formed horizontally but were broken, pushed upward and laid diagonally by movements of the salt of the lowest (and so, oldest) layer of the so-called Zechstein-period. The vertical line stands for a drill in the *Oberland* in 1938: for geologists, data from this drill confirmed the existence of the various rock layers.

The German word *Görtel* may be translated as "gutter" and stands for a relatively low area just west of the modern west coast where the Zechstein salt masses almost reach the surface.

The layers, from old to new:

Su, so, sm	= *(German)* Buntsandstein	= *sandstone*
Mu, mm, mo	= *(German)* Muschelkalk	= *shell lime (limestone)*
Cu	= *(German)* Unterkreide	= *Lower Cretaceous*
Co	= *(German)* Oberkreide	= *Upper Cretaceous*

(drawing from Ahrens, *Vorgeschichte des Kreises Pinneberg und der Insel Helgoland*, 1966, adjusted for English readers)

A brief geological history of Heligoland

Some 230 million years ago - during the so-called Zechstein period - the area of the present south-eastern North Sea was covered by another sea in a hot climate. The entire sea evaporated, leaving behind a deposit of hundreds of metres of salt. Many millions of years later, this "rock salt" would become mobile and cause the "birth" of Heligoland, as will be described below.

Between about 230 and 220 million years ago sand – or rather dust - was deposited upon this salty plain. This deposition could continue, because the land was slowly sinking. The lowest sand layers were compressed by the higher ones, thus slowly forming the presently visible sandstone layers. When studying pieces of broken red sandstone, geologists often find salt crystals or ribbled surfaces that must have been formed by streaming water, indicating that part of the sandstone was not only formed underground but also under sea cover. The distinctive red colour is caused by iron oxides inside the sandstone; the same oxides also cause the solidity of the sandstone. The layers of white *Katersand* are the result of wind deposits during periods when the area was dry[7].

Between about 220 and 210 million years ago shell lime (German *Muschelkalk*) – the oldest parts of the limestone complex – was deposited on top of the red sandstone. The shell lime was formed on the bottom of a shallow tropical sea with many creatures including shells; after the creatures had died, they slowly transformed into shell lime. The shell lime contains many fossils that can still be found on Dune Island[8].

In the Heligoland area we do not find any deposits of the so-called Jurassic period, from about 210 and 135 million years ago. Geologists do not have a definite explanation for this phenomenon. There are roughly two possibilities:
- the Jurassic deposits were somehow removed entirely;

---

[7] In past centuries *Katersand* was used by the islanders as material on the floors of their houses; the *Katersand* was taken away at spots where parts of the cliffs had fallen down.

[8] Most stones can be collected on the eastern pebble beach of Dune Island: for some 95% these stones are flints from the younger Upper Cretaceous Period.

- as a result of movements of the "rock salt" Heligoland already existed as an area above its surroundings during the Jurassic period, so that Jurassic deposits could not take place. Afterwards, Heligoland must have sunk, allowing younger deposits. Afterwards, Heligoland must have risen again.

Some 135 million years ago Cretaceous depositing of gypsum and chalk marl started. In the meantime the salt of the Zechstein period started drifting and lifted up all younger deposits. Some 50 million years ago Heligoland came to the surface. The highest points were reached where the upward drift of the salt was the strongest, in a weak point in the earth's crust, in the west of the area *Helgoländer Felssockel*. As the upward drift was less strong further to the east, the entire rock complex was laid diagonally.

It is difficult to imagine early Heligoland, even for experienced geologists. No doubt, early Heligoland was many times larger than the present *Oberland* and *Felswatt* together, perhaps the area of the present *Helgoländer Felssockel*. The top may well have been higher than now, however, we will never be certain. Almost certainly, the rock complex was steeply rising at the west side and sloping down towards the other side. Perhaps, in the beginning limestone and chalk layers were still lying on top of the sandstone ones. Further to the east – i.e. at present Dune Island – the limestone came to the surface later and that is why the *Wittkliff* was above sea level before 1711.

Once Heligoland had emerged, its rocky components started to erode by rainwater, seawater, ice, wind and vegetation, thus reducing Heligoland's size and height.

During some Ice Ages, Heligoland was covered with glaciers causing a relatively high degree of erosion. Thanks to the glaciers, the *Oberland* became an almost completely flat area. The glaciers also deposited new rocky material in the Heligoland area, originating from various parts of Scandinavia; nowadays, some of those "erratic" rocks can still be found.

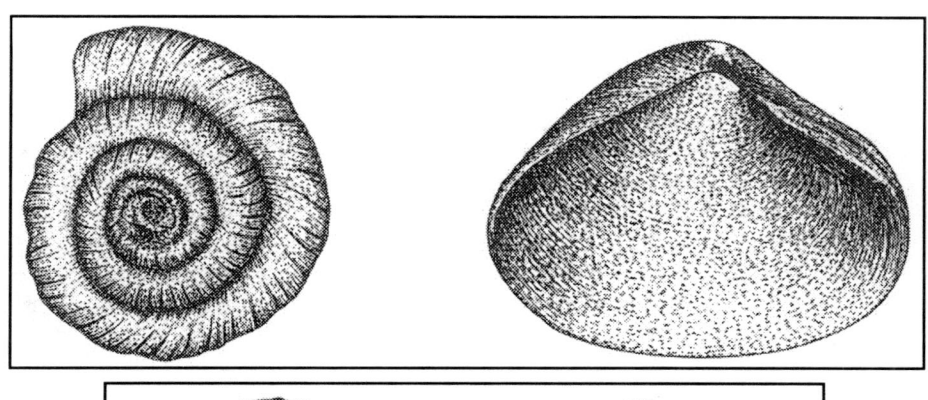

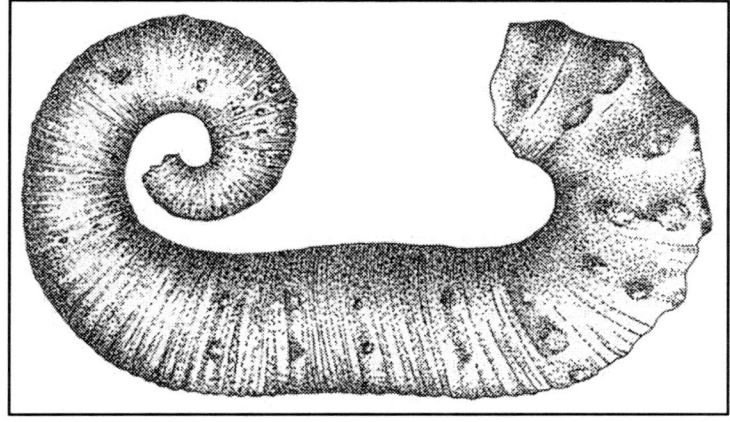

Three examples of Heligoland fossils dating from the Lower Cretaceous: in the upper left Rotularia phillipsii, *in the upper right* Thracia phillipsi *and below an example of the genus* Ancyloceras.

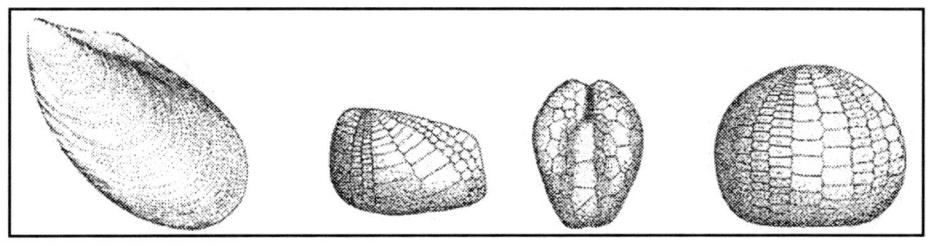

Examples of fossils from the Heligoland Upper Cretaceous: to the left we see the fossilised shell Inoceramus labiatus. *In the middle we see two views of the irregular sea urchin* Infulaster excentricus *and to the right a more "regular" sea urchin of the genus* Echinocorys.

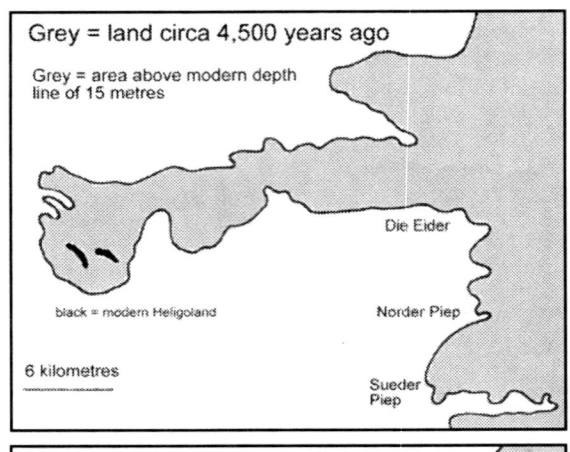

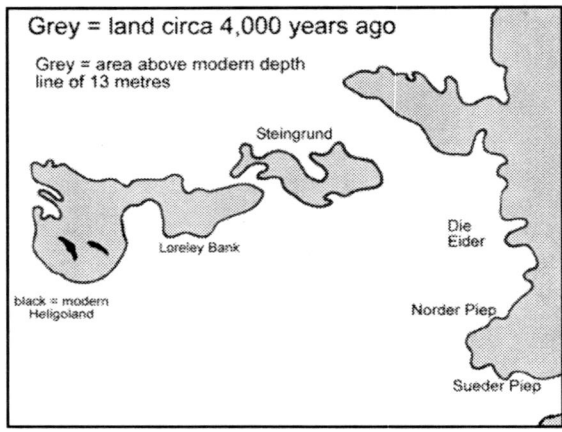

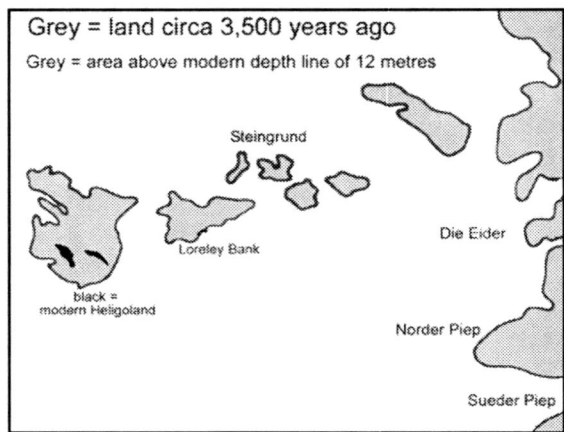

Possible development of the sea level: Steingrund *is a stony sea-bottom area outside the* Helgoländer Felssockel *(from CD Alt Helgoland in 2260 Bilder and Pratje, 1948*, Die Stadien in der Entwicklung der Insel Helgoland, Erdkunde 2, *pp.322-340).*

Heligoland after the last Ice Age: archaeology of Stone Age Man

During the last Ice Age, much of the bottom of the present North Sea was dry and was inhabited or at least frequently passed by Man (see the illustrations on the previous page). For example, in the Dogger Bank – about 150 kilometres northwest of Heligoland with local depths of only 13 metres – fishing nets are still bringing Stone Age artefacts to the surface nowadays. Regrettably, archaeological remains on Heligoland are scarce. In the 19th century some burial mounds – some of which may have been three metres in height – were still visible on the *Oberland*. Excavations of some of these mounds showed skeletons and artefacts.

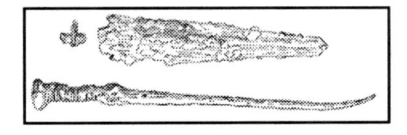

Artefacts (weapons) found in burial mounds on the Oberland (from C.Ahrens, Vorgeschichte des Kreises Pinneberg und der Insel Helgoland, 1966).

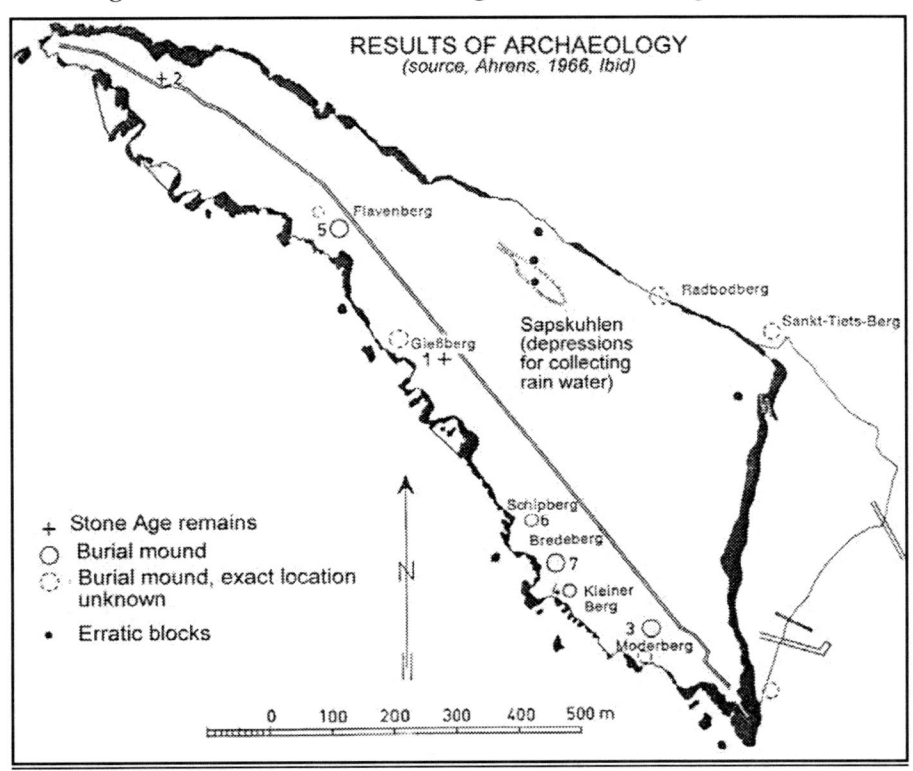

The mysterious copper plates

In the 1970s Heligoland's civil engineer Hans Stühmer – *the* expert in the island's geology until today – was diving close to South Harbour, to the southeast of the *Oberland* and made an astonishing discovery at a depth between 8 and 10 metres: a huge number of artificial *copper plates*, more or less circular with diameters up to about 100 centimetres!

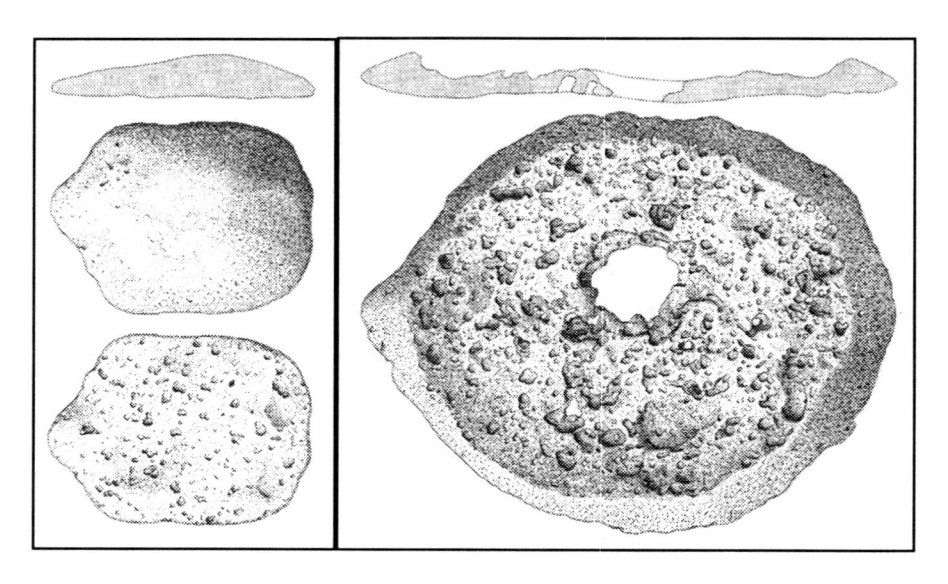

Drawings of two of the mysterious prehistoric Heligoland copper plates (up to one metre in diameter) (from periodical OFFA, nr.35, Wachholtz Verlag, Neumünster, 1978). Some real ones are in the Heligoland Museum.

Of course, Stühmer and others tried to explain this unexpected discovery. Could the plates be the remains of a shipwreck or have been thrown overboard from some ship in trouble? This explanation was very unlikely, especially because of the extremely high number of plates. Moreover, the copper happened to be polluted with Heligoland sandstone, indicating that the plates might have been made on the *Oberland*. Almost certainly, the plates had been manufactured close to the spot where they were found, indicating that there was once a part of the *Oberland* in what is now water with a depth of 8 to 10 metres!

Could the loss have been the result of an ordinary storm flood? This was not very likely, because in that case survivors would probably have tried to salvage some of the valuable plates. However, so many plates lay so close to each other that we almost have to conclude that there were no survivors. The most likely – and very spectacular - explanation is that the copper mining stopped suddenly as a result of some catastrophic loss of a large part of the south of the *Oberland*. The catastrophe must have been caused by sudden movements of the salt and gypsum layers underneath Heligoland. This catastrophe must have led to a *tsunami*-like wave in the North Sea; many of its shores must have been damaged to a much larger degree than any ordinary storm flood has ever done.

How old are the copper plates? In the 1970s researchers measured radioactivity from organic material on the plates and concluded that they had been made between about 1140 and 1340 AD. This was a surprising result, because contemporary chronicles neither mention copper mining on Heligoland nor a catastrophe resembling a *tsunami*. Later researchers made more accurate measurements of the radioactivity and so we now know that the plates must have been made many centuries earlier, almost certainly before the people around the North Sea could write, which could explain the lack of written evidence of a *tsunami*. Of course, the origin of the copper plates is still very mysterious and hopefully we will find out more in the nearby future.

The north point in the 19th century, before the construction of the protective wall (from Müller, Helgoland, 1977 (first edition 1882)).

Erosion by the waves

About 3,000 year ago the sea level reached its modern level and it has hardly changed ever since. Heligoland was an island now, subject to erosion by the waves. At the time, the Oberland was much larger than now. When the waves slowly removed the rocks above sea level, the present *Felswatt* (rocky tidal flat) slowly took shape. The waves created beautiful formations, especially at the island's west and north coasts, such as grottos and narrow peninsulas with arches at the bottom. When such an arch collapsed, a stack remained. However, since the construction of a protective wall along most of the west coast around 1900, erosion by the waves has diminished. This is one of the reasons why we see only one large stack today, the *Lange Anna* (Long Anna), resulting from the collapse of a natural arch in 1868.

The west coast in the 19th century, before the construction of the protective wall (from Gätke, Die Vogelwarte Helgoland, 1987 (reprint of 1900).

Mörmers Gatt (cave and arch) in Wehl, Ganz Helgoland (1996, first edition 1861) before its collapse in 1865.

Human activities that formed the present landscape

Of course, human activities have been highly responsible for the development of the Heligoland landscape. The following historical facts are important:

- before the bombardments during the Second World War, the *Oberland* was a flat area with the prehistorical burial mounds as the only upheavals. Furthermore, there were some artificial depressions for collecting rain water, the so-called *Sapskuhlen*[9];
- around 1650 the *Wittkliff* – located slightly north of present Dune Island - was still about as high as the sandstone plateau, with a size of about 10 hectares. A sand area connected the two cliff areas and there were sand dunes south of the *Wittkliff*. Both the *Wittkliff* and the sand area were slowly eroded by the waves. Besides, parts of the *Wittkliff* were taken away in order to be used on the mainland[10];
- on 1 November 1711 a storm put an end to the *Wittkliff*;
- on 1 January 1721 a storm split the island into the main island and Dune Island. In later years Dune Island was subject to heavy erosion (see picture below);

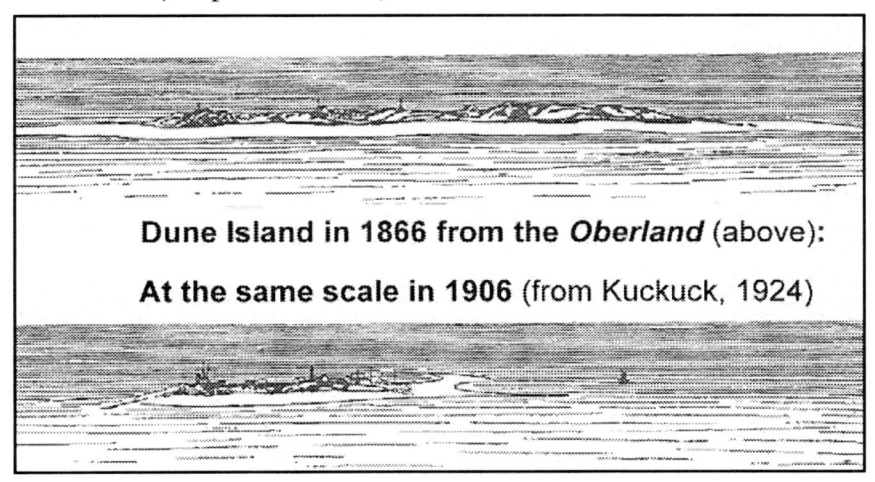

Dune Island in 1866 from the *Oberland* (above):

At the same scale in 1906 (from Kuckuck, 1924)

---

[9] Nowadays, the only preserved *Sapskuhle* houses the *Fanggarten*, the bird-catching garden.

[10] For setails, see pp.57-8.

- since around 1900 concrete walls have protected most of the western cliffs from large-scale erosion by the waves;
- around 1900 engineers started building South Harbour that got its present form around 1916;
- in the late 1930s the Nazi regime ordered – for military reasons - the creation of the *Nordostland* and an enlargement of Dune Island[11];
- during the Second World War (1939-1945) both islands were heavily bombarded and between 1945 and 1952 the British used both islands for military exercises. As a result, we now see many craters on the *Oberland*, formerly an almost flat area;
- on 18 April 1947 – the day of the "Big Bang" - British military detonated an enormous amount of explosive material in the south of the *Oberland*. As a result, the present *Mittelland* came into being, an area resembling a volcanic explosion crater.

Perhaps the salt masses underneath Heligoland are still slowly lifting the island upwards. However, for centuries the process of erosion has been of much more importance than the possible persistence of the upward shift. And so, Heligoland is slowly broken down to sea level. The stack and tourist attraction *Lange Anna* will no doubt fall down one day, in spite of the many efforts to keep it upright; in 1979 the *Lange Anna* even got a concrete wall around its bottom parts. In the 1980s a viewpoint only some 20 metres south of the *Lange Anna* had to be closed to the public because the location had become too dangerous.

In the end of November 1981 the south-eastern sandbar of Dune Island – called the *Aade*, meaning "tail" – was removed in a heavy winter storm. Around the same time, the eastern shore of Dune Island was only some 20 metres east of the airstrip. Since that time, Dune Island has grown in eastern direction, mainly with material from the island's own southern and northern beaches. In fact, Dune Island can only keep its present size by a continuous policy of adding sand, planting helm and up keeping the dams.

---

[11] For details see pp.95-96.

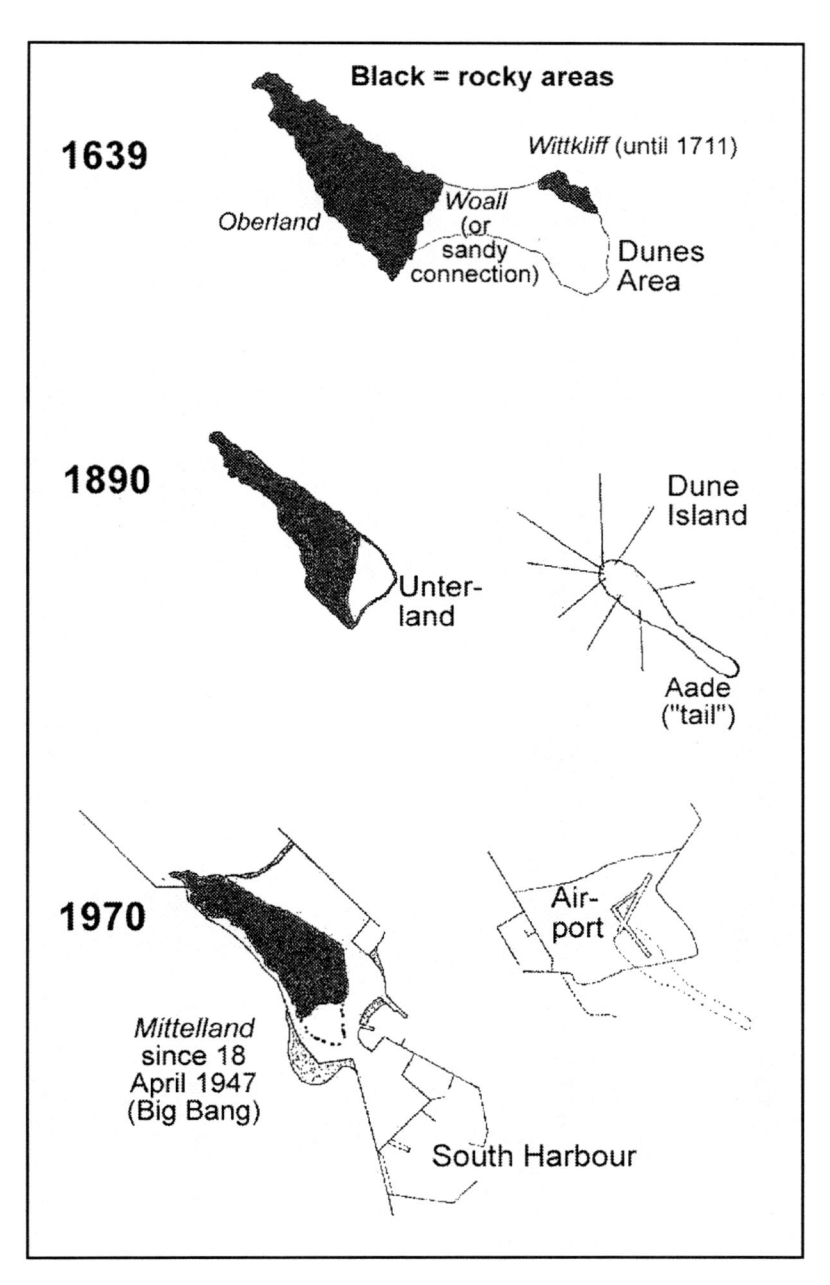

Heligoland in 1639, 1890 and 1970: the last two maps were drawn from a pamphlet of the Heligoland Museum; the other is drawn (and adjusted) from a map from 1639 by Johannes Meijer. In 1639 the Oberland *was undoubtedly larger than in 1890 but it is not possible to check the accuracy of the map of 1639; the size of the* Oberland *might be exaggerated.*

CHAPTER 3. Wildlife

Heligoland has a great wildlife. As a result of the rocky ground, botanists can find unique "endemic" species of plants here. Birdwatchers visit Heligoland in all seasons, e.g. in summer for the breeding seabirds and in autumn and spring for rare migratory birds. The annual booklet *Ornithologischer Jahresbericht Helgoland* ("ornithological annual report Heligoland") reports all observed bird species - and their estimated numbers - in a certain year, often some 250 species! Not very surprisingly, Heligoland houses a bird-ringing station (*Vogelwarte Helgoland*) and a biological centre (*Biologische Anstalt Helgoland*).

Mammals: rabbits and seals

Apart from pets and the – very interesting - sheep and cows on the *Oberland* the only land mammal is the **Rabbit** (*Oryctolagus cuniculus*, German *Kaninchen*), occurring on both islands. The beaches of Dune Island are often filled with hundreds of seals. The **Common Seal** (*Phoca vitulina*, German *Seehund*) may have many different colours. Males are up to two metres long, females up to one and a half metres. Pups are born in early summer and they often swim with their mothers a few hours later. The **Grey Seal** (*Halichoerus grypus*, German *Kegelrobbe*) is about 50 percent larger than the Common Seal.

Common Seal (left) and Grey Seal (photos by the author from placards on Dune Island).

Remarkably enough, Grey Seal pups are born in December and early January and stay on land in their first month. The females can be fertilized immediately after having given birth – and every bull wishes many females for himself! These magnificent scenes are a good reason to visit Heligoland around Christmas!

To the left a Razorbill, to the right a Gannet (by Anneke de Vries, from photos by the author).

Grey Seals (by Anneke de Vries, from photos by the author).

Cliff-breeding seabirds (five species) (see illustration on opposite page)

Five seabird species breed on the cliffs of Heligoland. Let us have a closer look at them.

The **Kittiwake** (*Rissa tridactyla*, German *Dreizehnmöwe*, c.7,000 breeding pairs in 2006) is a gull with a length of c.40 centimetres that makes a sound like *kie-ie-wake*. Like most gulls the upper parts are grey and the down parts are white. The bill is dull yellow and the feet are black. Both parents guard the usual three eggs.

The **Guillemot** (*Uria aalge*, German *Lumme* or *Trotellumme*, c.2,400 breeding pairs in 2006) has a length of c.40 centimetres with brown upper parts, white down parts and a thin, dagger-like bill. A female generally lays one egg, which is taken care of by both parents. When a chick is about six weeks old – and not yet able to fly -, it makes its renowned "Guillemot's jump" (German *Lummensprung*) into the sea, where it is fed by its parents for some more weeks. The "Guillemot's Rocks" (German *Lummenfelsen*) on Heligoland's west coast are *not* protected by a concrete wall, in order to allow the chicks their *Lummensprung*! The Guillemot should not be confused with the **Razorbill** (*Alca torda*, German *Tordalk*, about fifteen breeding pairs in 2006). The Razorbill has black upper parts and a distinctive bill: hooky and black with white lines. A female generally lays one egg, which is taken care of by both parents.

The **Fulmar** (*Fulmarus glacialis*, German *Eissturmvogel*, c.100 breeding pairs in 2006) has a length of c.50 centimetres. Inexperienced birdwatchers might confuse this species – with its grey upper parts and white down parts - with a Gull. The Fulmar has a remarkable "tube" on top of its yellow bill.

The **Gannet** (*Sula bassana*, German *Basstölpel*, c.190 breeding pairs in 2006) has an extraordinary length of some 90 centimetres. It is white with yellow on the top of the head and black at the tips of the wings. A pair generally has only one chick. On Heligoland, Gannets started breeding in the 1980s and their number is still increasing.

Lesser Black Backed Gull
(breeds on Dune Isl.)

Gannets

Fulmar

Kittiwakes

Guillemots

Fulmar

Razorbill

Kittiwakes

Razorbill

Guillemot

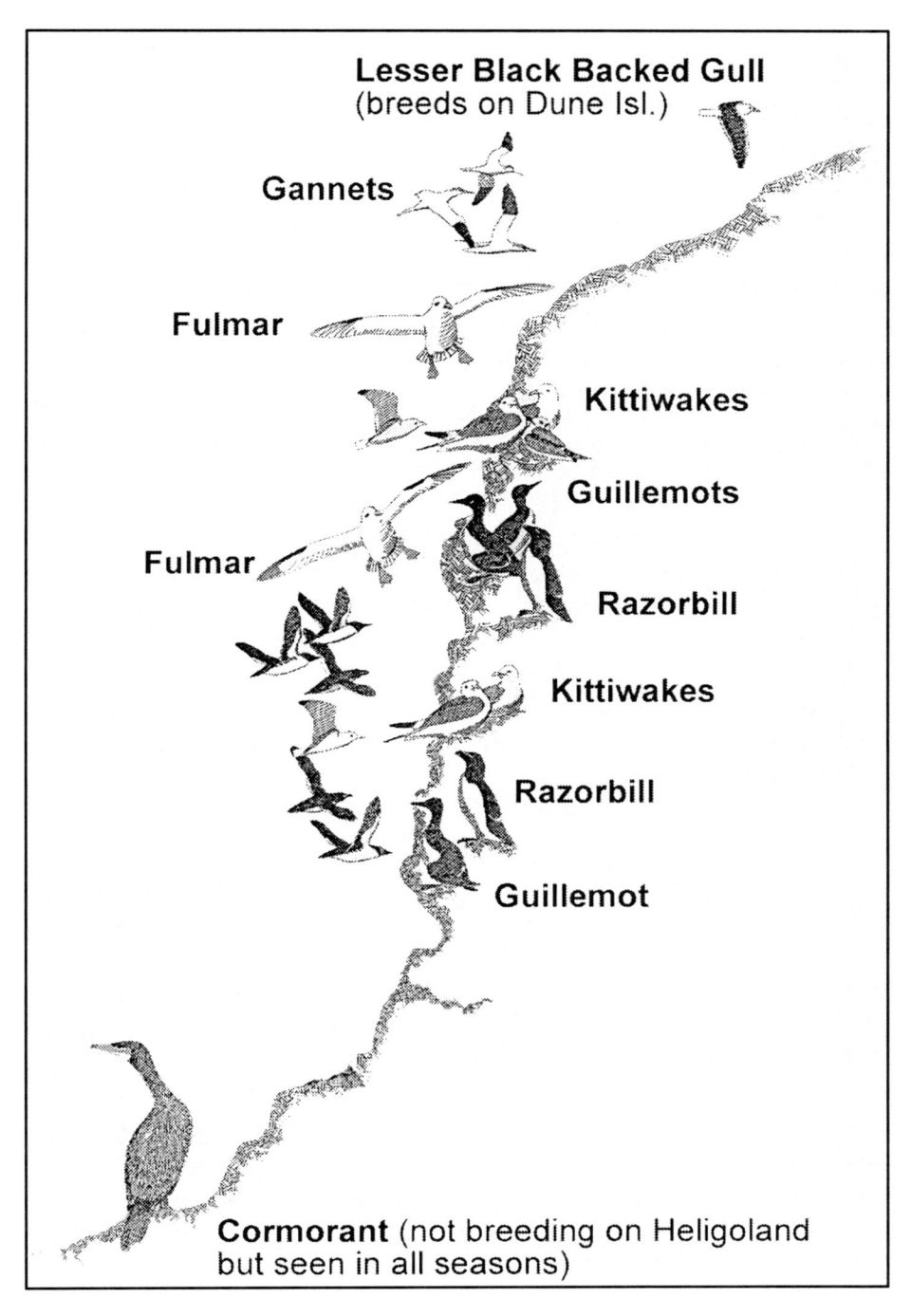

Cormorant (not breeding on Heligoland but seen in all seasons)

From Sören Sörensen, Vogels van de Noordatlantische eilanden, *1993, adjusted.*

*Guillemots (*Uria aalge*) (from Gätke, Ibid).*

Kittiwakes (Rissa tridactyla) *(juveniles are partly black) (from Gätke, Ibid).*

Other breeding birds, year-around birds and summer birds (selected)

Apart from the five cliff-breeding seabirds, both islands are also important breeding spots for other species of seabirds and waders and even a few landbirds. Evidently, all these breeding species also nest on nearby islands and mainland shores. For example, there is a beautiful colony of **Lesser Black Backed Gulls** (*Larus fuscus*, German *Heringsmöwen*) to the east of the Airport on Dune Island. **Herring Gulls** (*Larus argentatus*, German *Silbermöwen*) breed on various places on both islands. Other breeding birds include **Oystercatchers** (*Haematopus ostralegus*, German Austernfischer), **Ringed Plovers** (*Charadrius hiaticula*, German *Sandregenpfeifer*) and **Eider Ducks** (*Somateria molissima*, German *Eiderente*).

An immature large gull (the juveniles of the Lesser Black Backed Gull and the Herring Gull are almost similar) eating a crab (by Anneke de Vries, from a photo by the author).

An Oystercatcher (by Anneke de Vries, from a photo by the author).

A few bird species visit Heligoland in all seasons although they do not breed there: an important example is the **Cormorant** (*Phalacrocorax carbo*, German *Kormoran*) that is often seen in huge numbers.

In spring and summer you might you might also see various species of **Terns** (scientific family *Sternidae*, German *Seeschwalben*), resting and feeding around Heligoland, although they breed on the nearby German and Danish shores.

Bird species outside the breeding season

Outside the breeding season, Heligoland is an important "port of refuge" for many bird species. For example, in winter you can observe various species of **Geese** and **Ducks** (scientific family *Anatidae*, German *Gänse* and *Ente*). On some winter days Heligoland is invaded by **Common Buzzards** (*Buteo buteo*, German *Mäusebussarde*).

Most international bird watchers come to Heligoland in spring and autumn when migratory birds are passing Heligoland and often make a short stop in order to feed and rest. Many of these birds are generally classified as seabirds or waders but the number of species of land birds is much higher. Land birds can not rest or feed on the North Sea unless they meet a ship or Heligoland!

The activities of the Vogelwarte

The *Fanggarten* (Bird-catching station) is located in a former *Sapskuhle* - a depression to collect rainwater - on the *Oberland*. As it is enclosed by a wall with a height of some two metres, the *Vogelwarte* is overlooked by many visitors, however, it is well worth visiting; in the tourist season, there are guided tours a few times a week.

Small birds crossing the North Sea and landing on Heligoland are often attracted by the man-made oasis with plants and fresh water ponds inside the former *Sapskuhle*. And before they realise what is going on.... they are trapped! Fortunately they are not killed but they are in hands of humans for a few moments. After the workers have ringed the birds and have registered species, age (if possible), gender (if possible), weight and length of the wings, they are released at once. On some days – especially in spring and autumn – the number of birds inside the *Fanggarten* is 800! Of course, these data are processed in numerous scientific researches. For example, most land birds in the *Fanggarten* have systematically less weight than birds caught on the mainland. In fact, this result is not very surprising; it proves that most land birds reach the *Fanggarten* with an empty stomach!

The Fanggarten *(by Anneke de Vries, from a photo by the author).*

An important example of a *breeding* land bird is the **Blackbird** (*Turdus merula*, German *Amsel*). The Blackbird (length c.25 centimetres the male is black and the female is brown) is one of the most common birds in northwest Germany but the isolated position of Heligoland offers an excellent opportunity to investigate the lives of these birds. And so, workers of the *Vogelwarte* (Bird Station) try to ring and track all birds, nowadays about 60 breeding pairs, including one pair on Dune Island. A male may have several females but the chicks of some of his females may not be his!

The underwater world

Heligoland's marine world has, of course, many resemblances with the underwater world of the rest of the North Sea. However, the rocky underground houses a lot of extra species of animals and plants, namely species that dislike sandy or muddy grounds: one of those species was once caught for commercial reasons, namely the lobster (*Homarus gammarus*, German *Hummer*). An excellent exhibition of the marine life can be seen in the *Helgoland Aquarium* in the *Nordostland*.

At low tide, the upper parts of the underwater world can be seen on the tidal flats of both islands. Of course, the north beach of the main island and all beaches of Dune Island beaches offer excellent opportunities for collectors of seaweeds and shells, especially after storms.

The Felswatt *(rocky tidal flat) near the north point at very low tides: the* Nordmole *(northern dam) is not shown (from Olaf Goemann,* Echt Helgoländer Hummer, *1990): 1=cliff edge, 2= Guillemot's Cliffs (German* Lummenfelsen*), 3=rubble fallen from the cliffs, 4=high water line at the foot of the cliffs, 5=Stack* Lange Anna, *6="lake" at low tide, 7=gutter at low tide*

Ten Heligoland shells, from left to right, their sscientific names: Turritella communis, Natica catena, Mactra stultorum, Littorina obtusata, *both sides of* Cardium edule, Littorina littorea, Donax vittatus, Mya arenaria, Trochus zizyphinus, Scalaria communis *(from Kuckuck's* Nordseelotse*)*.

Rocky undergrounds offer living space for Barnacles, blue mussels, brittle stars and much more (from Olaf Goemann, Echt Helgoländer Hummer, *1990).*

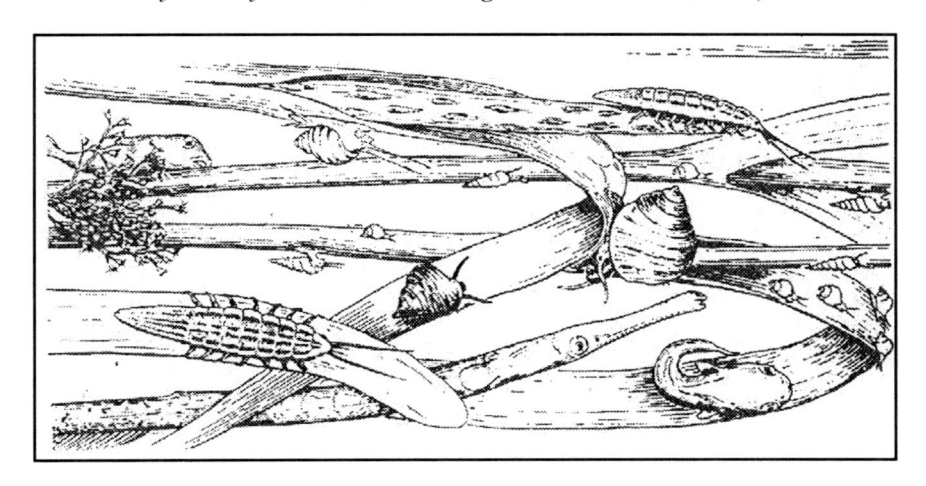

Algae offer protection to Isopoda, Gastropoda, Syngnathidae and several young fishes (from Olaf Goemann, Ibid*).*

Plants and flowers

Both the main island and Dune Island are good spots for botanists, because of the unique soils and the salty and hardly polluted air. In summer many parts of the *Oberland* turn yellow from the **Wild Cabbage** (*Brassica oleracea*, German *Klippenkohl*). Cultivated plants often grow wild on Heligoland, so that sub-species arise. For example, you can find wild sub-species of **Beet** (*Beta vulgaris*, German *Rübe* or *Zuckerrübe*). Other plants include types of **Hogweeds** (genus *Heracleum*, German *Bärenklau*), **Mayweed** (*Tripleurospermum maritimum* but also *Matricaria perforata*, German *Echte Strandkamille*) and **Sea Milkwort** or **Sea Milkweed** (*Glaux maritima*, German *Strand-Milchkraut*).

As the winter temperatures on Heligoland are significantly higher than on the adjoining mainland, island gardens may have Mediterranean species, such as the **Black Mulberry Tree** (*Morus nigra*, German *Maulbeerbaum*) that can be seen in the garden of the *Haus am Maulbeerbaum*. This tree was planted around 1770 and survived the bombardments during and after the Second World War! It is now a tourist attraction.

*Above a **Sea Holly** (Eryngium maritimum, German Stranddistel), below a **Burnet Rose** (Rosa pimpinellifolia, German Dünenrose) (from Kuckuck, Ibid).*

CHAPTER 4. Legends of saints and pirates (c.700-c.1600)

There are many interesting stories about Heligoland's early history, however, those stories generally comprise a mix of facts and legends.

The name Heligoland may well come from "Holy" land; in modern German and Dutch "holy" is spelled as *heilig*. Let me start with describing some legends from the early Middle Ages about holy people on the rock.

Around 700 AD: Legends of saints on Heligoland [12]

Around the year 692 – when most people in the north of present Germany were not yet Christians - the holy Willibrord reached Heligoland, then called Fositesland. The pagan islanders worshipped a holy well and a number of holy cows. The islanders were shocked when they saw that Willibrord drank from the holy well and killed some holy cows. The islanders were astonished when the saint did not get his expected terrible punishment. Obviously, the holy well and the holy cows were just as normal as other wells and cows! Finally, Willibrord was not hindered in his converting activities.

Around the year 718 the holy Wulfram came to Heligoland and saw that two boys were selected for some pagan sacrifice, probably dedicated to the sea-god Aegor or Ekke. The boys were left behind at a sand bank at low tide in order to be drowned by the rising tide. Wulfram pleaded for the lives of the boys before the pagan king, who answered that the boys would be for Wulfram if Wulfram's God would save them. And then a miracle occurred: the tide stayed below its usual level and Wulfram led the two boys into Christianity.

---

[12] Sources: Hubrich-Messow, *Sagen und Legenden von der Insel Helgoland*, 2004, pp.39-41 and Fiedler, *Helgoland*, 1988, pp.16-17.

Around 1050 AD: bishop Eilbert on Heligoland

A Latin account by one Adam of Bremen, who wrote about 1072, was often thought to refer to Heligoland but it is not more than a legend, although a very beautiful one. The following summary is by W.G. Black in *Heligoland and the Islands of the North Sea* (1888):

> (…) Eilbert was sent on a mission to Funen by Archbishop Adalbert of Hamburg, who flourished 1034-1072, but was captured by pirates and taken to Farria, an island at the mouth of the Elbe, but hidden in the wide seas, scarcely eight miles in length and four in breadth. The inhabitants used straw and wreckage for fuel. The legend was current that pirates who carry the slightest booty from the island – either shipwrecked goods or those of a slain man – never would reach their home again in safety; therefore the pirates, with the utmost care, always paid over a tithe of their plunder to the lonely hermit who lived in the island. The island was fruitful, rich in birds, and afforded good pasturage for cattle; it had one tower, no trees; was surrounded by steep rocks, and had one approach, near where the sweet water (the holy well) was. The place afforded safety to ships, except from pirates. For this reason the island was called the Holyland.
>
> Interesting as this account is, and closely as in many respects Adam of Bremen's account corresponds to what we may safely regard as the state of things in Heligoland in the eleventh century, there are two points in which he has clearly either confused two stories, or must be taken to be writing of a different island. Farria was never a name for Heligoland; it was the name of the Faroe isles. Heligoland was almost certainly in 1072 not so large as he represents. Yet the Faroe islands are certainly not at the mouth of the Elbe (….)

1400s and 1500s: pirates on Heligoland, legends and facts

Tradition has it, that between about 1396 and 1402 pirates such as Klaus Störtebeker and Goedeke Michel used Heligoland as their base point. No doubt, in those days there were *really* pirates in the North Sea, hunting for the numerous merchant ships with valuable cargo. However, legends and facts are sometimes difficult to distinguish. Let me tell one legend that is definitely not true. When Störtebeker and his men were taken prisoner and sentenced to death by the City of Hamburg, Störtebeker would have saved the lives of some of his comrades in a remarkable way. After he had been beheaded, Störtebeker walked along some of his comrades before finally falling down. As agreed, the comrades that Störtebeker had passed were set free!

In reality, we have no documentary evidence about pirates living on Heligoland at all. For example, the *Bolzendahl* Chronicle tells about many roundups and executions of pirates between 1401 and 1578, especially by the city of Hamburg. According to this Chronicle Klaus Störtebeker and his men were captured in the neighbourhood of Heligoland in 1401 but this does not mean that Störtebeker and his men ever lived on the island. In fact, it is not very likely that pirates like Störtebeker and Michel ever lived on Heligoland for many years. If they had done so, the pirates would have made things very easy for their enemies. It is far more likely that the pirates had ever-changing hiding places on other islands. The high rock of Heligoland was perhaps a good *rendez-vous* point for ships including pirate ships but that is something else.

In popular writings, pirates like Störtebeker and Michel were a sort of Robin Hoods, stealing from the rich and giving to the poor. However, the real story is not so romantic. In reality, pirates were often "privateers" who had got an official "permission" to pirate the enemy; that permission came from noblemen or kings who had written so-called *letters of marque* for that purpose. When the kings or noblemen did not need their privateers any more and the privateers could not - or did not want to – return to a civil life, they often became pirates and a threat to anyone.

Another doubtful but entertaining story about a pirate on Heligoland is the story of pirate Wieben Peters from Dithmarschen (on the mainland to the east of Heligoland, in present Holstein). In 1545 Peters and some of his comrades would have been killed in the church of Heligoland after a long hunt by a mob of Dithmarschen people. The Dithmarschen and the Heligolanders would have celebrated this victory with barrels of beer that were on board the Dithmarschen fleet! It is not unlikely that Wieben Peters *really* existed and was *really* killed by his own Dithmarschen countrymen but it is very likely that chroniclers decided to enhance the story somewhat!

About 1530: a legend about the conversion to Lutheranism & the Monk Stack [13]

Around 1530 the islanders - as most people in northern Germany and Scandinavia - converted from Roman Catholicism to Lutheranism. One legend tells that the new religion was introduced to the islanders by a man who had been a Catholic monk. When the man landed upon the island and started promoting the Lutheran religion, the islanders were not interested and threw the former monk from the southern cliffs. Next night the ghost of the monk rose as a stack resembling a monk at the same spot he had fallen into the sea; so the renowned stack The Monk came into being. With a voice of thunder, the stack summoned the islanders to accept the new religion. The stack did not become silent until the last islander had become Lutheran. It is said that in later days the stack made a warning when an islander had been naughty.

The Monk Stack, once standing near the southern tip of the Oberland. *On 18 April 1947 the south of the* Oberland *and the Monk vanished, because of an enormous explosion by British military (from* The Graphic, *17 November 1877).*

---

[13] Source: Hubrich-Messow, *Ibid*, pp.12-13.

How the herrings disappeared [14]

The erratic mating behaviour of herrings has caused many economic ups and downs for Heligoland and numerous other coastal spots in northwestern Europe. For example, huge herring catches around Heligoland were reported in 1425 and 1753 but they did not last forever. There are at least two legends about the behaviour of the herrings in the Heligoland waters.

Once huge numbers of herrings came very close to the island every spring. At high tide the herrings even landed upon the street. The islanders used tons of salt to preserve the valuable fishes. One day, a woman had run short of salt and became so reckless that she started sweeping the herrings back into the sea. That was a mistake, because the herrings stayed away, leaving the islanders in terrible poverty.

Another legend tells that each year, in early spring, the islanders were carrying a crucifix around the island in a solemn procession, leading to good herring catches every year. But one year, while the usual round was only half traversed, came a cry that the herrings were in sight. At once, all men went to their boats and the bearer of the holy relic let it fall and it was broken. A number of good women brought the broken pieces to the church but the punishment for this blasphemy could not stay away. And so, the herrings did not come back.

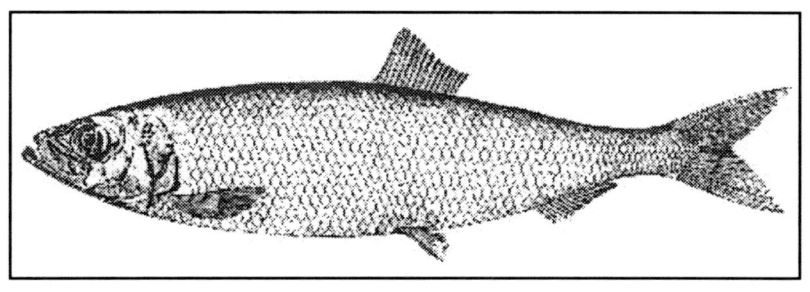

*Herring (*Clupea harengus, *German* Hering*) on a 19th century engraving (http://www.gma.org/fogm). Salted herrings were people's food in Europe until far in the 18th century.*

---

[14] Sources: W.G.Black, *Ibid*, p.21, Hubrich-Messow, *Ibid*, pp.17-18.

CHAPTER 5. Socioeconomic history (until c.1940)

As a result of its location, Heligoland often had a turbulent political and military history. Heligoland was owned by several powers:
- until 1544 by Hanseatic cities, the Duchy of Schlewsig-Gottorp and the Kingdom of Denmark (see chapter 6);
- 1544-1684 by Schleswig-Gottorp (see chapter 6);
- 1684-1689 by Denmark (see chapter 6);
- 1689-1714 by Schleswig-Gottorp (see chapter 6);
- 1714-1807 by Denmark (see chapter 7);
- 1807-1890 by Britain (see chapter 8);
- since 1890 by Germany (see chapter 9).

The islanders, however, always remained Heligolanders (part of the Frisians) who had to make a living from their tiny land and its surrounding seas. This chapter deals with the major socioeconomic themes throughout the ages:
- the island's "council" until 1868 and the connected *Bürlott*-system (a sort of communal financial system and social security);
- piloting to mainland ports;
- wrecking and lifesaving;
- fishing and hunting birds and seals.

The island's council and the Bürlott-*system, c.1500-1868*

Between about 1500 and 1868 the most important Heligoland men were those who possessed a so-called *Bürlott*, i.e. those who paid island taxes on private land and houses. A man from overseas who married a Heligoland woman was allowed to stay on the island but would never get a *Bürlott*. Who had a *Bürlott* could claim part of the revenues from wrecking and piloting. When a man owning a *Bürlott* died, his widow generally became the new owner. In fact, the *Bürlott* system functioned as a sort of social security; even the island people without a *Bürlott* were taken care of if they got ill or old. For modern historians it is almost impossible to get a complete insight in the internal financial affairs of the island in former days. Contemporary outsiders generally did not really understand the affairs either. For example, we read in a tourist guide for Heligoland printed in 1856:

> I have never been able to find out whether the pilot revenues flow into some communal treasury or that the revenues are distributed. It is difficult to find out the laws and customs of the island anyway, even after having stayed here for many years[15].

The island council or "parliament" was an oligarchy, its members being male *Bürlott*-owners. The council's composition and its way of election hardly changed over time. As an example, let us take a closer look at the situation around 1810 when the number of male *Bürlott*-owners was possibly about 200. The island's affairs were run by six Magistrates, who in turn nominated seven Quartermasters and sixteen Aldermen. The tasks of the Quartermasters included commanding pilot boats and other craft engaged in public service and keeping clean the streets in their "Quarters". The Aldermen acted for the Quartermasters in their absence. Together, all Magistrates, Quartermasters and Aldermen formed the *Vorsteherrschaft*, which assembled so rarely that it did not even have a meeting-house[16].

The island council dealt with various economic and legal cases, in co-operation with the deputy that the overlord – the Duke of Schleswig-Gottorp or the monarch of Denmark or Britain – sent to the island. In many cases the overlord did not interfere too much with the island's affairs – although the authorities from Schleswig-Gottorp and Denmark generally levied taxes for their own treasuries.

---

[15] *Die Lustfahrt nach Helgoland*, 1987, p.29. Author of this tourist guide was Karl Reinhardt. See also page 80.

[16] George Drower, *Heligoland – The True Story of German Bight and the Island that Britain Betrayed*, 2002, p.34.

Piloting to mainland ports [17]

In times past there were no reliable sea maps, buoys, beacons and lighthouses to indicate the safe sea-routes. And so, large ships bound for Hamburg, Bremen or other ports needed the experienced pilots of Heligoland or their rivals from nearby places as Hamburg and Blankenese.

In the 15th and 16th centuries every Heligoland boatman having a *Bürlott* (i.e. who paid the island taxes) was allowed to offer his piloting services. For that purpose, the boatmen cruised around the island, hoping to meet a ship's captain needing their services. In 1587 it was stated that the piloting services should not be offered before the ship had anchored. In 1640 "free cruising" was allowed again, especially as a reaction to a freely cruising ship from Hamburg with many rival pilots on board.

From about the middle of the 17th century *pilot examinations* were compulsory. From then on, not every boatman was allowed to call himself a pilot any more. The examinations consisted of dozens of questions – about the mouth of the Elbe, the mouth of the Weser, etc. - that the candidates had to answer correctly.

Heligoland pilots could be away from home for weeks. Firstly, the sailing time from Heligoland to Bremen, Hamburg or other destinations could be several days. Secondly, after having done their service, the pilots often had to wait long for an opportunity to get back home.

Around 1790 there were some 300 Heligoland pilots who piloted some 400 ships a year. In 1843 the number of pilots was about 350. From about 1860 onwards, the number of Heligoland pilots diminished, as a result of better sea maps and an increasing number of buoys and lighthouses marking the shipping lanes. In 1890 the number of pilots was only 194. The last examination was carried out in 1923.

---

[17] Krüss, *Fischer – Schiffer - Lotsen*, 2003, pp.33-40.

Official Heligoland Pilot's Signs, made of messing. One side always showed the sovereign and the other side showed a pilot man and the number of the pilot. From left to right the weapons of King Christian VII of Denmark (ruling years over Heligoland 1766-1807), King George III of Britain (ruling years over Heligoland 1807-1820), both sides of a sign under Queen Victoria of Britain (ruling years over Heligoland 1837-1890). In the final right we see the sign of Kaiser Wilhelm II (ruling years over Heligoland 1890-1918).

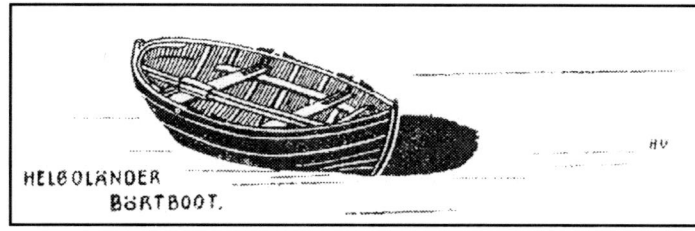

Two typical Heligoland boats, a Börtboot *and a* Schaluppe *(All pictures on this page from* Kuckucks Nordseelotse, *1924).*

Wrecking and lifesaving

It is hardly exaggerated to state that the Heligolanders – as other island and coastal people – needed shipwrecks for their livelihood. The wrecks supplied the islanders with wood, meat, wine, coins, and so on.

The old laws and regulations of wrecking and lifesaving are very complex and confusing. Moreover, it is difficult to find out to what extent those laws and regulations were carried out. For example, in the 16th century and before, the old Frisian laws stated that all foreign survivors of shipwrecks were… slaves or prisoners that had to pay for their freedom!

In the old days the products washed ashore went into the pockets of those who found them. Both the overlord and the island council often tried to institutionalise wrecking practices, simply because both regarded wrecking as a source of revenue. Neither the overlord nor the islanders cared much about the property rights of the rightful owners.

In 1559 Duke Adolph II of Schleswig-Gottorp (ruling years 1544-1586) made a "Heligoland Strand Regulation", although it was perhaps a confirmation of an already existing practice. According to this regulation, the islanders were allowed to take over a stranded vessel three tides after the stranding, provided it had not been able to get free on its own. Not very surprisingly, the Duke claimed half of the revenue.

In past times no man was supposed to shirk his responsibilities if a wreck came in sight. In other words, every man had to help with salvaging and lifesaving. The salvaged goods were stored in specific huts on the *Unterland*, so that partition could be carried out in an orderly way[18].

When a ship had got stranded, an island boat came and the islanders told their salvage charge. If the captain found the charge too high and thought

---

[18] Michael Herms, *Flaggenwechsel auf Helgoland – Der Kampf um einen militärischen Vorposten in der Nordsee*, 2002, p.24.

he could do the work himself, the islanders went away. When the ship did not move, the islanders often came back a few hours later. If salvaging had become more difficult or dangerous in the meantime – because of darkness, tides or bad weather – the islanders now demanded a higher salvage charge! Indeed, the salvage charges were dependent on the degree of danger or difficulty! As a result, there were often captains of ships stranded near Heligoland who complained about their treatment by the islanders until far in the 19th century.

Traditionally, wrecking, salvaging and lifesaving were closely connected to piloting – also because the same men carried out the work. It should be mentioned that the islanders generally did their best to save the lives of the persons on board the unfortunate ships; there are even cases in which the rescuers lost their own lives.

In 1820 the island council – supported by the British Governor - made a remarkable and unpopular decision: the *Bürlott*-shares for salvaged goods were abolished. All revenues from stranded vessels had to be given to the communal treasury and the workers were paid for their labour only[19]. In 1868 Coast Guards, in the British style, were established, in order to guard the interests of the rightful owners of the wrecked ships.

A wreck on the rocky tidal flat off the west coast (from The Graphic of 17 November 1877).

---

[19] Krüss, *Ibid*, 2005, p.16.

Fishing[20]

Fishing has, of course, always been very important for the islanders, both for direct consumption and for export to the mainland. Important species of edible fish included mackerel (*Scomber scombrus*, German *Makrele*), haddock (*Melanogrammus aeglefinus*, German *Schellfisch*), cod (*Gadus morhua*, German *Kabeljau* for adults and *Dorsch* for juveniles) and whiting (*Merlangius merlangus*, German *Wittling*). Cod and whiting were often used as winter stocks, after having been either salted or dried in the wind. Herring (*Clupea harengus*, German *Hering*) was caught around the island as well but the results varied enormously, because this fish species often changes its breeding grounds.

In summer Northern sandlances (*Ammodytes dubius*, German *Sandaale* or *Sandspierlinge*) were caught with nets near Dune Island, in order to be used as baits for larger fishes. During the rest of the year other baits had to be used, such as the livers of oxen and seals.

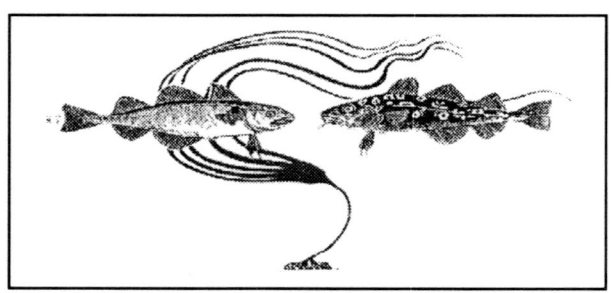

Left to right a haddock, an underwater plant (the species Laminaria digitata*) and a young cod (from* Kuckucks Nordseelotse, 1924*).*

Heligoland is the only place in the southern North Sea with lobsters (*Homarus vulgaris*, German *Hummer*), because lobsters prefer rocky bottoms. Lobsters were usually caught from early April to the end of October. Around 1780 the first lobster pots came to Heligoland, probably imported from Scotland. As lobsters live only on very distinctive spots, the traps had to be placed with large accuracy: The right spots were identified by using landmarks on both islands. Around 1890 a

---

[20] The entire paragraph about fishing is derived from Krüss, *Ibid*, 2003.

new lobster spot was found some ten kilometres to the east, on the so-called *Steingrund* (literally "stone ground"), where the exact placing of the traps was, of course, more difficult.

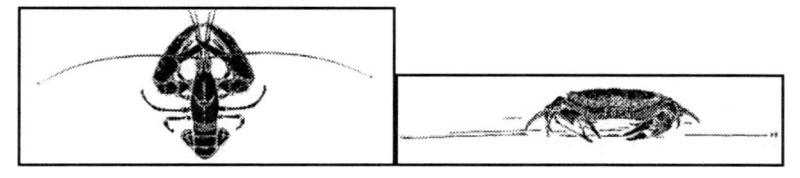

Lobster (left) and Edible Crab (from Kuckuks Nordseelotse).

Lobsters could be sold at high prices on the mainland. For example, in the 1930s four island fishermen were wholesale traders in lobster as well. The animals were transported alive in order to keep them as fresh as possible. Lobsters were also consumed on the island itself, especially served to tourists in restaurants. Since the Second World War the number of Heligoland lobsters has gone down sharply; the precise reasons are unknown. Fortunately, the modern tourist can eat *Knieper* - the claws of the "edible crab" (*Cancer pagurus*, German *Taschenkrebse*) – in many restaurants.

Lobster pots (from Müller, Helgoland, *1977 (first edition 1882)).*

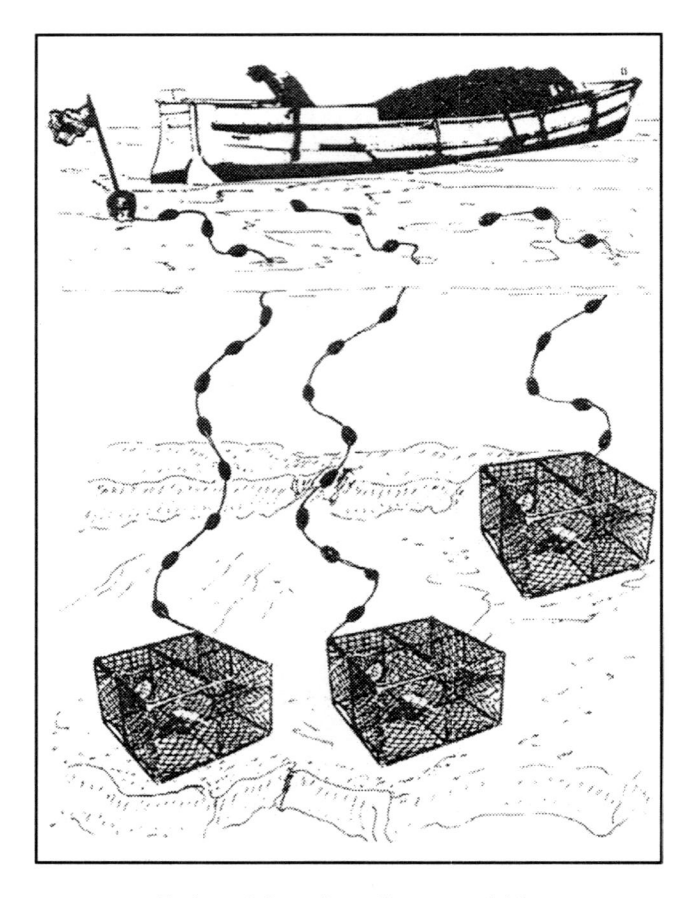

Lobster fishing (from Goemann, Ibid*)*.

Hunting seals and birds

As on other European shores, on Heligoland seals were hunted for their hides, meat and oil until far in the 20th century. For example, seal livers were used as baits for fishing. Moreover, until only a few decades ago seals were considered unwanted competitors for the fishermen.

Birds were hunted to a degree that we still see in southern France and Italy nowadays. Birds were often served in a soup, for instance, thrush soup (German *Drosselsuppe*) was a real delicacy. During spring and autumn hundreds of migratory birds could be caught in one day, using huge nets. A highly wanted migratory bird was the Woodcock (*Scolopax rusticola*, German *Waldschnepfe*), because it fetched high prices on the mainland. An extraordinary catch seems to have been made on 21 October 1823: more than 1,100 Woodcocks![21] Nocturnal hunting was often done near the lighthouse, because it was – as other lighthouses – often surrounded by wounded, confused and slowly moving birds. Of course, *breeding* birds were hunted as well; for catching cliff-breeding seabirds – or their eggs - men and boys had to make acrobatic acts, as is still done in Iceland and the Faroe Islands. No wonder, the numbers of breeding birds on both Heligoland islands have risen since large-scale hunting ceased some decades ago!

In the 19th and early 20th centuries tourists hunted birds and seals as well. And so, many islanders rented weapons and provided boat trips to the game hunters.

Left: net and lamp of a Heligoland bird hunter. Right: In spring and summer, some species of terns (family Sternidae, German Seeschwalben) often rest and feed on Dune Island (both pictures from Kuckuck, Ibid).

---

[21] Kuckuck, *Der Nordseelotse*, 1924, p.243.

CHAPTER 6. Heligoland under the Hanse and Schleswig-Gottorp, c.1400-1714

c.1400-1544: various disputes about Heligoland

As Heligoland is located close to the mouths of the important rivers Weser, Elbe and Eider, Heligoland was an important port of refuge for merchant and fishing ships. In 1425 and subsequent years the island's importance increased further because of the extraordinarily large harvests of herring that were made around the island. According to W.G. Black in *Heligoland and the Islands of the North Sea* (1888) Heligoland would remain the principal station for the herring fisheries for over 200 years, until the herring crossed the sea again to the Scottish coast[22].

After 1425 Heligoland was wanted by the King of Denmark, the Duke of Schleswig-Gottorp and Hanseatic cities like Bremen and Hamburg. The following – although incomplete and somewhat confusing – data from the chronicles clearly show the importance of Heligoland:

- in 1427 the Duke of Schleswig rented the island to the Hamburg capitalist Heine Brand;
- in 1433 the Danish King appointed a deputy on the island;
- a document of 1435 is probably the eldest mentioning a church on the island. A document of 1436 shows that the church belonged to the bishopric of Schleswig;
- in 1439 the Danish King rented the island to the Hamburg capitalist Heine Brand (the same man had been mentioned in 1427);
- in 1444 disputes were recorded between islanders and Frisians and people from Dithmarschen (located in what is now western Holstein);

---

[22] Black, *Ibid*, p.18.

- in 1463 Hamburg people took away material of Heligoland's *Wittkliff*, the first record of a long list of quarrying activities[23];
- in 1470 the Duke of Schleswig gave the island to the Cathedral of Schleswig but a few years later the island was property of the Duke again;
- around 1490 the Duke of Schleswig decided to impose a duty on the fishery of Heligoland. Of course, the duty irritated merchants from Hanseatic cities as Bremen and Hamburg;
- in 1496 troops of the Duke burnt down the island's storehouses, belonging to Bremen merchants;
- in 1497 the island was captured by a coalition of the Hanseatic cities Hamburg, Bremen and Stade that destroyed the ducal buildings. The cities got help from many men of Dithmarschen. However, the ducal troops soon retook the island;
- in 1498 a new Hanseatic attack was hindered by ducal troops;
- in 1499 Hamburg and the Duke agreed to an armistice, leading to the exchange of many prisoners. The Dithmarshen people continued their struggle against Denmark and Schleswig;
- in February 1500 Dithmarshen troops defeated Danish ones in the Battle of Hemmingstedt, leading to an armistice on 15 May of that year.

In 1544 the island became once again part of the Duchy of Schleswig, a situation that would last until 1684. In 1565 the Duke tried to sell the island to the Lutheran Church – without success. The Dukes often tried to make money from their colony, e.g. by taxing pilot's services, claiming part of the value of stranded ships or even directly taxing boats.

A few islanders went far from home and got in trouble. For example, in 1679 a Heligoland ship in the Mediterranean was captured by pirates who sold the crew as slaves in Algiers. The crew got home after ransom money had been collected on the island; the islanders had to pay 2,100 Thaler for the captain alone[24].

---

[23] For more details, see the next paragraph.
[24] Krüss, *Chronologie der Insel Helgoland*, 2005, p.10.

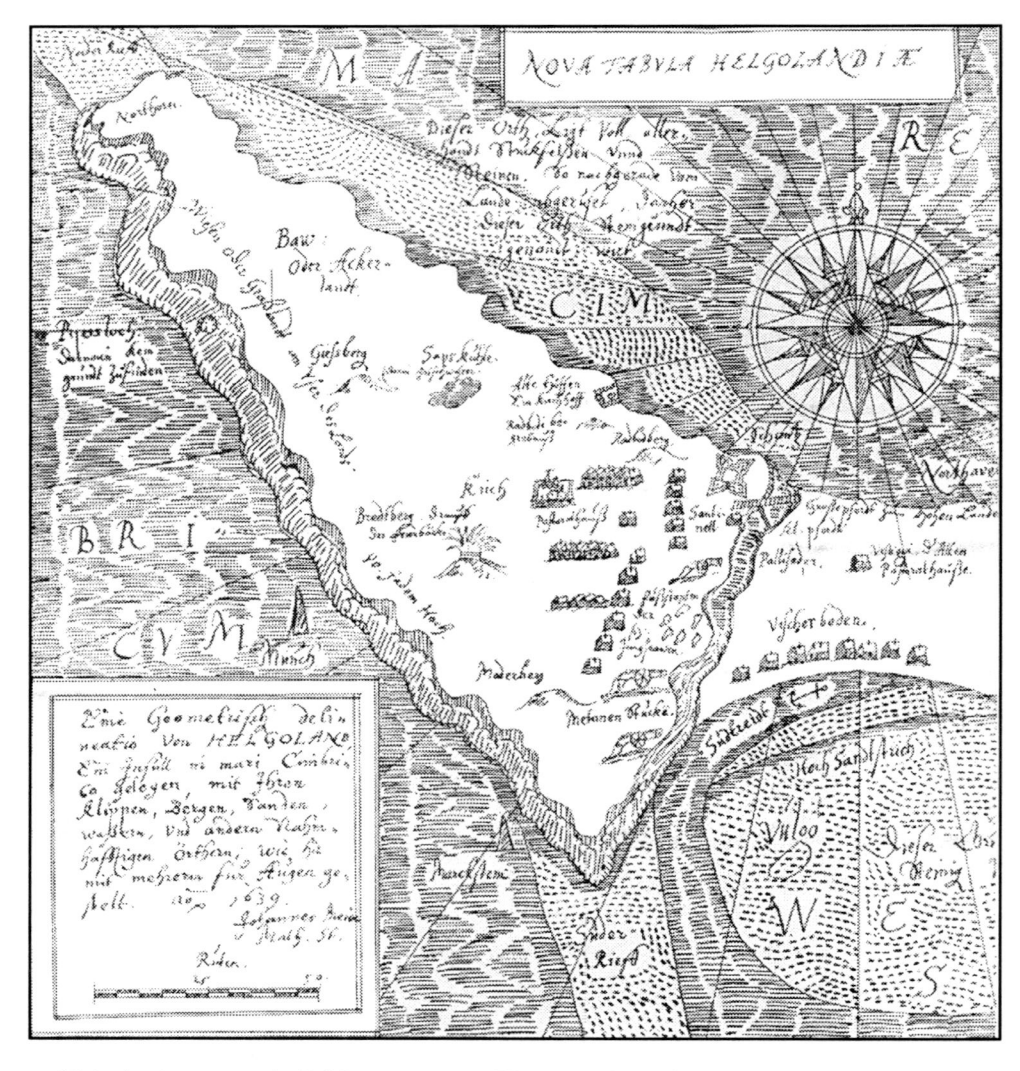

Heligoland on a map by J. Meijer in 1639. We see a military fort in the northeast of the Oberland and three guns on the eastern edge of the Oberland (from Ahrens, Ibid, 1966). In the Unterland we see huts used to store fish and things from wrecks. Further to the east (not on this picture) we find the Wittkliff and the south-eastern dunes.

c.1463-c.1650: the quarrying of the Wittkliff

From the middle of the 15th century until far in the 17th century many parts of Heligoland's eastern *Wittkliff* were taken away in order to be used on the mainland: chalk marl (German *Muschelkalk*) could be used as building material and other materials could be used in large ovens. The orders for the materials came from town magistrates or – more often - from the Dukes of Schleswig-Gottorp. Research in the 20th century showed that at least one ducal castle in Tondern (nowadays in Danish Schleswig), built around 1544, was partly built with material from the *Wittkliff*. We do not know to what extent the quarrying of the *Wittkliff* – that was subject to natural erosion as well - attributed to its final disappearance in 1711.

This map of 1650 clearly shows the Wittkliff *in the northeast and sand dunes in the southeast, connected to the* Oberland *by a low sand area.*

Many authors of the 18th, 19th and 20th centuries wrote that the islanders themselves had been active in quarrying the *Wittkliff* but in 1992 August Wilhelm Vahlendieck, in his superb book *Das Witte Kliff von Helgoland*, put an end to this legend. After he had studied many documents – often bookkeeping accounts of companies - in archives, Vahlendieck proved that various companies, often located in Hamburg, carried out the quarrying work and transport. The work was done by non-Heligoland workers and the stones were transported to the mainland by non-Heligoland ships.

Regrettably, we have no contemporary records about the reaction of the islanders to the removal of part of their tiny land. However, it seems likely that they were disappointed but that they did not have the power to prevent the quarrying activities of the mighty overseas powers.

Lighthouses in the 17th and 18th centuries [25]

In 1630 a first lighthouse, a coal fire on the *Oberland*, started operating. Its location was close to the location of the present lighthouse but closer to the western cliff edge. Tradition has it, that the islanders were not amused and generally refused to co-operate, because they were afraid of losing income from piloting and wrecking! Moreover, the islanders were afraid that the fire could endanger nearby island houses. The islanders even refused to carry the coal to the *Oberland*!

Remarkably enough, the first lighthouse seems to have been made in order to fill the Ducal treasury. The Duke paid half the building costs and also paid part of the upkeep costs but he also claimed half of the so-called "fire money" or "fire duties" (German *Feuergeldern*) of one *shilling Lübisch* per "Last", to be paid by ship's owners in Hamburg, Stade, Bremen and all ducal ports. In 1637 the light was discontinued, especially because the costs remained higher than the benefits.

In 1676 a new coal fire started operating. This second lighthouse was run by the City of Hamburg. To keep the fire going, high-quality coal from Scotland was imported: in the beginning, some 180,000 kilograms a year for a price of about 10,000 *Reichstaler*! The lighthouse was not used during about four months in spring and summer. In 1761 it was decided to use the lighthouse throughout the year and so the amount of used charcoal rose to almost 500,000 kilograms a year!

---

[25] Information from *Die Küste*, 1990, pp.86-88.

A modern artist's impression of the former coal fire (from Die Küste, *1990).*[26]

1684-1689: *Heligoland is temporarily Danish*

In 1684 a Danish admiral approached Heligoland. At night his men captured Heligoland fishermen. The admiral sent a message to the island stating that the captured fishermen would be imprisoned or even killed unless the island would be surrendered. Tradition has it, that the women persuaded the weak Schleswig force to surrender.

Interestingly, after they had come to power, the Danish authorities tried to become friends with the islanders: the Danes promised to acknowledge the freedom of the islanders and even appointed an islander as governor. However, at the peace in 1689, the Danes returned the island to Schleswig.

---

[26] This coal fire remained functioning until 1810 when a new lighthouse started operating; the old building was then used as a signal tower. In 1916 it was broken down, so that a newly-built heavy German gun could shoot.

1689-1714: the final years of Heligoland under Schleswig-Gottorp

In 1689 Heligoland once again belonged to the Duchy of Schleswig-Gottorp. On 28 January 1696 the Ducal deputy included an interesting census in his official report[27]:

Men (*Einwohner in allen*)	163[28]
lower men (*Gesellen*)	58
Widows	93
Married women, maidens and children	646
Total	960 islanders

Apart from the 960 islanders, the island also housed the priest, the church servants and the military from Schleswig-Gottorp. The report also stated that of the 93 widows, 36 were dependent on alms, 22 were fed by their children and 35 ran their own household[29].

In 1698 Duke Friedrich IV ordered grain exports from Hamburg to Heligoland[30]. Obviously, the island production of grain, vegetables and other foodstuff was no longer sufficient to feed all people on the island.

As the amount of land available for farming was very small, regulations were necessary. Around 1700 the following regulation was made about the common meadow between church and *Sapskuhle* (a man-made depression on the *Oberland* containing drinking-water for animals and people). Owners of one-cow shares were allowed to place only one sheep from their own meadow into the common meadow[31].

---

[27] Otto-Erwin Hornsmann, *Geschichte und Geschichten der Insel Helgoland*, 2006, p.22.
[28] Probably the male *Bürlott*-owners, i.e. the men who paid the island taxes.
[29] The latter widows had probably inherited a *Bürlott*.
[30] Michael Herms, *Flaggenwechsel auf Helgoland*, p.25.
[31] Kurt Friedrichs, *Umkämpftes Helgoland*, 1995, p.19.

In 1707 the first staircase – a wooden one – between the *Unterland* and *Oberland* was constructed, perhaps because a better connection was considered necessary.

On 1 November 1711 a storm washed away the last remains of the *Wittkliff*. The low sandy connection between the sandstone cliffs and the eastern dunes still existed but was often overflooded during storm floods.

Accounts from a lieutenant, 1699

In 1699 one Lieutenant Böttcher was the highest military on Heligoland. He wrote very good and entertaining reports. A summary[32]:

- the animals drank from the *Sapskuhlen* on the *Oberland*. The water from the *Sapskuhlen* was red and "thick" and full with vermin. Nevertheless, this water was also used for cooking. Some fresh water came from wells in the *Unterland* and the low sandy connection with the dunes. However, the best drinking water was collected in the south-eastern dunes;

- the islanders sometimes cooked their fish but more often they ate dried or smoked fish. The islanders liked to drink beer from Husum in Schleswig with their fish meals. One would rarely meet an islander without a dried fish in his pocket;

- the boatmen were often two or three weeks away from home. During their absence they were often forced to eat less fish and more meat and they said to become sick from eating too much meat;

- fish-processing was done by women, mainly in storehouses on the *Unterland*, where one often saw and smelled rotting fish heads;

- when a married man died, his eldest son of 12 to 14 years could become the new chief of the household.

---

[32] Hornsmann, *Ibid*, pp.17-21.

CHAPTER 7. Heligoland is Danish (1714-1807)

1714-c.1720: A Danish raid and its aftermath

In the summer of 1714, during the so-called Nordic War, Denmark saw a new opportunity to attack the strategically important rock of Heligoland. As in 1684, the Danes started by capturing some island fishermen at sea. On 6 August 1714 the Danes landed on the eastern dunes that were still connected to the main island in those days. The Schleswig commander on the island evacuated the *Unterland* and mobilized male islanders but the Danish were too strong and bombarded many houses. The islanders were not willing to fight any more and two days later the Schleswig commander surrendered.

The Danes allowed the Schleswig troops to return home but the islanders were humiliated. For example, many island boats were confiscated and auctioned in Glückstadt. The islanders were deprived of their income from piloting ships to German towns, something that also disturbed some English merchants who had been good customers of the experienced Heligoland pilots[33].

In 1716, two years after the capture by Denmark, all male islanders were obliged to promise obedience to the Danish King, in exchange for a reduction of the Danish garrison; we do not know if the garrison was reduced indeed[34].

In later years, the Danish mitigated their occupation policy and reduced the number of Danish military. Moreover, the remaining Danish military were poorly armed and equipped.

---

[33] Rickmers, *Ibid*, p.21.

[34] Rickmers, *Ibid*, pp.20-21.

Events c.1720-c.1750

On 9 October 1719 many islanders witnessed an extremely rare event on the *Hingsgars* (horse meadow) on the *Oberland*: the public beheading of an island woman who had slain another woman. For this purpose, an executioner from Glückstadt had travelled to the island. A public execution was, of course, nothing unusual in Glückstadt, Bremen or Hamburg but this execution was the only one that has ever been recorded on the island[35].

On the night from 31 December 1720 to 1 January 1721, a heavy storm washed away the narrow sandy land between the main island and the eastern dunes. From that date, Heligoland has ever existed of two islands.

Sometimes the Danish authorities tried to make financial gain out of the islanders. For example, in 1739 the Danish king tried to introduce a new tax on piloting. As a result, many Heligoland pilots threatened to move to Wangerooge Island in order to continue their services from there. The king finally withdrew his plans[36].

Socioeconomic changes and disasters, c.1720-c.1800

The Heligoland population grew rapidly during the Danish period. In 1696 (under Schleswig-Gottorp) the population was only about 960 but in the middle of the 18th century the population was about twice as large[37]. Interestingly, in the beginning of the Danish period the population increased partly as a result of immigration of skilled manual workers such as ship's carpenters and sail-makers. Obviously, these workers were considered important for the island economy. The islanders also imported high-quality wood for shipbuilding from far-away Rhineland. The skilled workers coming to the island were, of course,

---

[35] Hornsmann, *Ibid*, p.31.

[36] Krüss, *Ibid*, 2003, p.34.

[37] In 1723 at least eight families seem to have tried to emigrate to Langeoog Island. However, they all seem to have returned to Heligoland (Hornsmann, *Ibid*, p.30 with the annotation about re-migration from Erich-Nummel Krüss).

always male and often married Heligoland women. At least ten soldiers of the Danish garrison did the same[38].

The few hectares of land were intensively used. For example, in 1726 the island council issued a remarkable and interesting regulation about the churchyard on the *Oberland*; it was stated that it was *not* to be used for grazing cattle, erecting bird catching nets, drying wash or drying fish, because the churchyard was a garden of God and because the dead should not be disturbed[39].

Some documents dated around 1733 give interesting information about church and school[40]. We read that the island had two Lutheran priests, who had to share the work equally; at any moment, at least one priest had to be on the island. The church also employed the schoolmaster. Children from six to fifteen (inclusive) had to attend the school that had to classes; in the first class the children learnt reading, in the second one also writing and calculating. It is not clear to what extent families could afford the school career of their children, because attending school was not free of charge.

Farming seems to have increased during the 18th century. For example, in 1736 a third *Sapskuhle* on the *Oberland* was made as a resource of rainwater. Between 1751 and 1799 the amount of cows went from 40 to 10, whereas the number of sheep went from 200 to 400. Other sources of food were goats, poultry and wild birds. Barley was grown on the main island and potatoes were grown on Dune Island[41].

Life could be very harsh. Smallpox often occurred on the island, causing 106 fatalities in 1751, 162 in 1768, 74 in 1784 and 90 in 1799. The miliary fever (German *Frieseln*) caused 145 casualties in 1757/58. A drinking water urgency occurred in 1798. Of course, there were also frequent casualties at sea. An extreme example occurred on 12 January 1773, when

---

[38] Hornsmannm, *Ibid*, pp.30-31.

[39] Friedrichs, *Ibid*, p.19.

[40] Hornsmannm, *Ibid*, p.32 and Friedrichs, *Ibid*, p.18.

[41] Herms, *Ibid*, p.29.

no fewer than 27 islanders drowned, when they were all on board a single ship sailing from Hamburg to Heligoland; most men were pilots who had involuntarily stayed in Hamburg or environment for weeks, waiting for an opportunity to return home. The 27 men left behind 24 widows and 63 orphans[42].

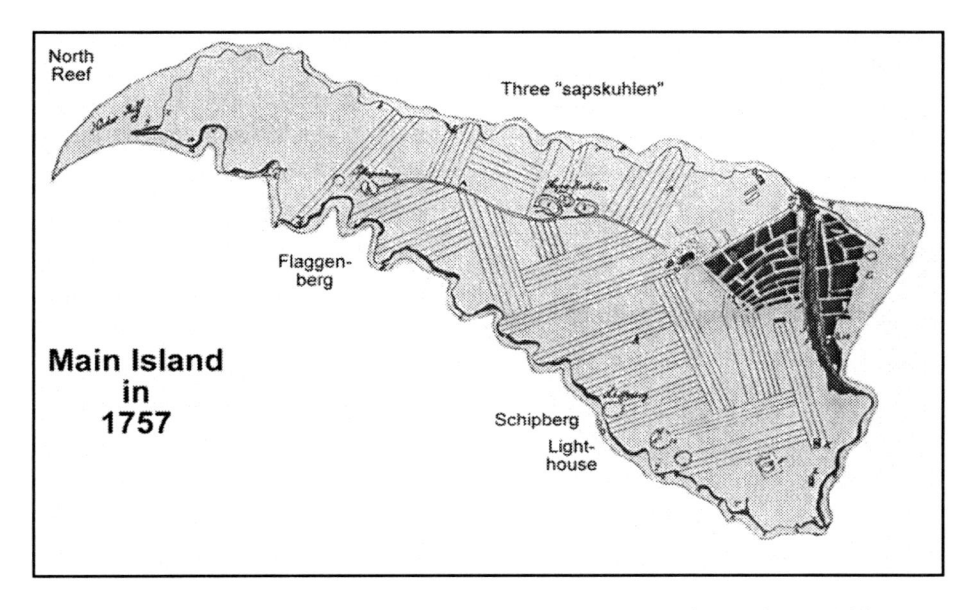

This map clearly shows intensive farming on the Oberland *(from Ahrens, Ibid).*

Fortunately, the rising of international commerce and shipping during the 18th century also increased the career opportunities for male islanders, some of whom became crew members, officers or even captains of large Danish or foreign ships. And so, some islanders embarked on Dutch and Hamburg whaling ships or on Danish merchant ships heading for Danish colonies in the tropics.

Fortunately, the Danish authorities sometimes did good things for the islanders. For example, in 1765/67 the Danes built and financed a new staircase to the *Oberland*. Regarding the intensive use of the *Oberland* this new staircase was probably by no means a luxury. In 1796 this staircase was replaced by a new one.

---

[42] Krüss, *Ibid*, 2003, pp.36-39 and Krüss, *Chronologie der Insel Helgoland*, 2005, p.13.

An eyewitness in 1793

Johann Friedrich Zöllner (1753-1804), a German clergyman and author of theological and geographical papers and schoolbooks, visited Heligoland in 1793. A short summary of his interesting account[43]:

- The Heligoland man was fisher and pilot, and little more. Teenage boys were hunting birds. The women did the rest: housekeeping, carrying things up and down the staircase, keeping the nets and angles in order and working on the fields;

- When a boatman went to Hamburg, other islanders often asked to do some shopping for them. After homecoming, he simply dropped the purchased things at the bottom of the staircase and the things were never stolen.

- The *Oberland* was monotonous, one part being covered with barley fields and the rest being pasture grazed by a few hundred sheep that ate every upcoming leaf[44];

- The island had no trees, except for a Black Mulberry Tree[45] in the garden of the priest, and a few trunks that had been planted shortly before;

- The lighthouse, run by the City of Hamburg, could be seen at a distance of four miles. In a long stormy winter night almost four thousand pounds of charcoal were used;

- All marriageable girls were equally rich and the bride's treasury was not more than a bed and a chest with "treasures" in it. The *Bräutigamsstand* (time between engagement and marriage) could last for years, during which boy and girl were allowed to see each other twice together with her parents. After marriage, the couple soon had many children. The elderly were taken care of;

---

[43] From *Die Lustfarhrt nach Helgoland*, 1987, pp.115-120.

[44] Zöllner must have seen the prehistoric burial mounds as upheavals on the *Oberland* but he did not write about them.

[45] German *Maulbeerbam* (*morus nigra*). The same tree is still there and nowadays the garden of the *Haus am Maulbeerbaum* is a tourist attraction. In contrast to the rest of northern Germany, Heligoland's winter temperatures are high enough for this tree to survive.

- On Sunday evenings with good weather the whole population gathered near the church, enjoying themselves with dancing and gaming.

Zöllner wrote somewhat idyllically; for example, he did not write about the frequent losses of lives caused by epidemics and storms. However, Zöllner also wrote that the islanders had to miss something:

> It is hardly surprising that the Heligoland women love the island, because most of them never see the mainland: for them, Heligoland is the entire world. They would never start thinking that things could be better elsewhere (...) However, the men are sometimes in Husum, Cuxhaven, Glückstadt, Stade, Bremen and Hamburg. Why don't they wish to exchange the island, where one has to make so many efforts to import products, for a place where those products are in abundance?

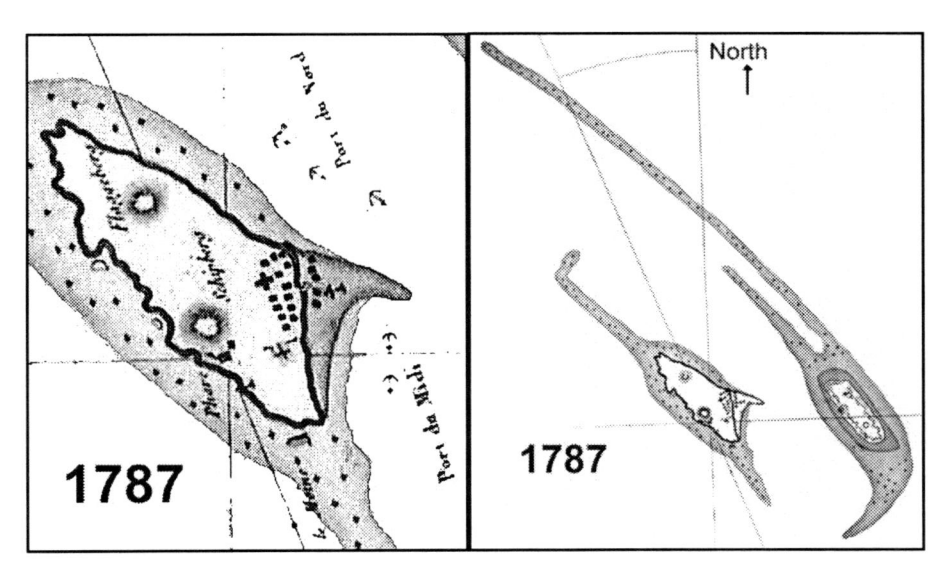

Part of a seamap showing Heligoland and its tidal zones in 1787 by the Frenchman J.B. Tardieu the Younger (from a photo by the author of a tourist placard – in the right one the text has been removed). We read six topographical landmarks for navigators: Port du Midi *(Middle Straits),* Port du Nord *(Northern Straits),* Moine *(Monk Stack),* Phare *(Lighthouse) and the prehistoric burial mounds* Schipberg *and* Flaggeberg. *Obviously, these mounds were high enough to be useful as navigation landmarks.*

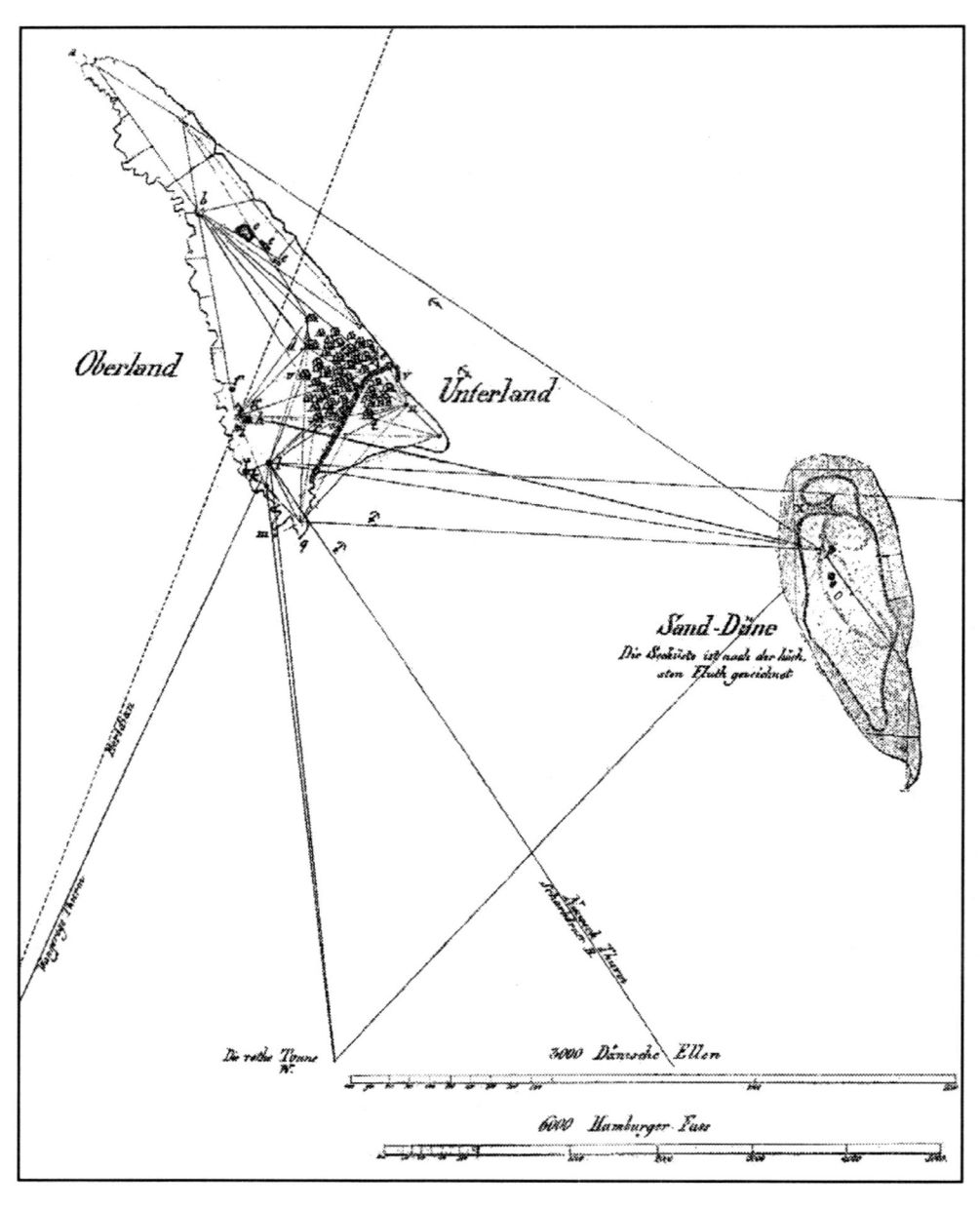

Map of 1793, supplied by the island museum. The large size of Dune Island - that is shown above the highest flood line – is very apparent. To the south of both islands we see Die rothe Tonne, *the red ton functioning as a navigation buoy.*

68

CHAPTER 8. Heligoland is British (1807-1890)

1807-c.1814: Heligoland becomes British and a smuggling centre

In 1807 Heligoland was once again a pawn in European warfare. In those days, the French emperor Napoleon wanted to isolate Britain by cutting off the latter's trade connections with mainland Europe. When in the summer of 1807 British spies informed London about a potential alliance of France with Russia and Denmark, the British authorities decided to carry out a pre-emptive strike on neutral Denmark, by destroying many Danish warships in Copenhagen[46]. Shortly afterwards, on 4 September 1807, a number of British warships anchored at Heligoland. One day later the Danish commander, Major Zeske, already surrendered. Zeske commanded no fewer than 206 men but they were poorly trained and armed[47]. During the following days, all prisoners of war were brought to the mainland and set free.

For Britain, the rock of Heligoland was now a strategic landmark, just as British occupations as Gibraltar and the islands of Malta and Capri in the Mediterranean. Heligoland was now the "Gibraltar of the North Sea"!

The immediate effect of the British occupation was bad for the islanders. As they had become "hostile foreigners", the islanders could no longer pilot to mainland towns. Moreover, the islanders lost their exports of lobster and fish to the mainland. The Danish authorities even confiscated some Heligoland boats. Moreover, the small island got overcrowded with hundreds of British military. During the winter of 1807-08 the British had to distribute imported food to the islanders in order to prevent massive starvation.

---

[46] Britain's actions were not without risk: in August and September 1807 Britain received war declarations from Russia, Prussia and Denmark (Drower, *Ibid*, p.5).

[47] The British had expected only one Danish officer and 25 soldiers – at least that was the information that some spy gave to the British authorities who finally decided to invade Heligoland! However, the prediction that the Danes would surrender early happened to be correct (Drower, *Ibid*, p.13).

One or two years after the British siege, Heligoland's economy started booming as a smuggling centre. Precious British and colonial products were stored on the island and smuggled into northern Germany. In 1810 the total value of products stored on the island seems to have been £ 20 million. A total of 300 to 400 ships a day calling and departing from Heligoland was no exception. The island seems to have been nicknamed "Little London"! The islanders rented land and buildings to the many British merchants at high prices. The Heligoland pilots – about 300 at the time - made fortunes by carrying out the dangerous but well-paid smuggling trips. Sometimes the Heligoland pilots came home with mainland men and boys willing to fight under British command. One of the best Heligoland pilot-smugglers was Claus Reimer; the Napoleonic authorities put the high prize of 300 Thaler on his head![48]

In 1810 the British lighthouse – a modern one for its time – was constructed. Around the same time, the *Falm* – the avenue along the southern edge of the *Oberland* – was paved.

The British lighthouse with the older coal fire to the right: the latter was used as a signal tower in the British period (from Wehl, Ganz Helgoland, 1996 (first print 1861)).

---

[48] Herms, *Ibid*, p.32.

In Spring 1811 the exiled King of Sweden, Gustav Adolf IV, stayed a few weeks on Heligoland; he was one of the many heads of state having lost his land during the turbulent Napoleonic wars. The ex-monarch donated two large silver candlesticks to the church, one of which is still in the present island church of St. Nicolai[49].

In 1814 the smuggling period came to an end, because Britain made peace with Denmark[50]. The storehouses became empty and the foreign merchants left. As a result, Heligoland soon fell into poverty.

1814-1863: the early British governors

After the smuggling period, the islanders tried to return to their former life. However, this was not easy. For example, as the islanders had become "British", they now had to pay import duties when they sold fish on the nearby mainland markets. The island pilots still piloted overseas ships to the mainland but the revenues were low as a result of fierce competition from other places.

With the consent of the British governor, in 1820 the island council (*Vorsteherrschaft*) abolished the *Bürlott*-shares for salvaged goods. All salvaging work and costs had to be paid by the communal treasury and all revenues had to be given to that treasury. The rescue workers were paid for their labour only[51]. This unpopular decision was made because the communal treasury could not be filled with traditional revenues any more.

In 1820 and 1821 the last British soldiers were removed. The only British people who remained were the governor and a few – probably less than ten – civilian employees. Without the military, the islanders now had to

---

[49] Krüss, 2005, *Ibid*, p.16.

[50] In January 1814, at the Treaty of Kiel, Heligoland was officially recognized as a British colony by Sweden and Denmark. However, the British gave back two other Danish islands, which they had conquered: Anholt to the east of Jutland and the Caribbean island of St Thomas. Obviously, the British diplomats considered Heligoland of great importance.

[51] Krüss, *Chronologie der Insel Helgoland*, 2005, p.16.

maintain law and order themselves. And so, in January 1822 the island council – with the consent of the governor – installed a Civil Guard, consisting of six islanders, including one officer[52].

No doubt, the most important event in the early 19th century was the start of tourism with the opening of the *Seebad Helgoland* in the summer of 1826. Next paragraph will be dedicated to this phenomenon but let us first take a closer look at the early British governors, all of whom had the interests of the islanders in their minds.

In contrast to Denmark, Britain never demanded a tribute from the islanders and the Colonial Office in London even paid the costs for the governor and his staff. For example, in 1836 the total cost of the civil establishment's salaries on Heligoland, as paid by the Colonial Office were £ 963. In 1848 they were £ 1,023, specified as follows[53]:

Governor	£ 500
Clerk to Governor	£ 136
Two Clergymen, each £ 50	£ 100
Two Magistrates, each £ 30	£ 60
Town Clerk	£ 60
Signalman	£ 60 10s
Navigation bosun	£ 33 6s 8d
Mail Carrier	£ 69 6s 8d
Keeper of the Blockhouse	£ 3
Total	£ 1,022 3s 4d

The early governors William Osborn Hamilton (1808-1815), Henry King (1815-1840) and John Hindmarsh (1840-1857) were popular among the islanders because they hardly interfered with their daily life. And if they interfered, most islanders usually adhered the intervention. For example,

---

[52] Horsmann, *Ibid*, p.52.

[53] Drower, *Ibid*, p.35.

Governor King often lobbied for a doctor on the island, however, with changing success. In 1831 the same Governor reported to London that poverty on the island was worse than ever before. He wrote that he had ordered to break down some useless and decayed storehouses; the wood had been sold in order to fill the fund for the poor[54]. Under the same governor, a new staircase was built in 1834: with a few modifications, this structure remained upright until 1945. Governor Richard Pattinson (1857-1863) took the side of Heligoland's pilots, especially when they were unfairly accused by ship-owners of hazarding vessels in the River Elbe[55].

The island authorities sometimes made unorthodox decisions. For example, in the mid-19th century an islander who had been sentenced to three years in prison was released on the condition that he and his family would emigrate to America. The island treasury paid the trip to America, because that was cheaper than taking care of the family for three years![56]

The staircase in the middle of the 19th century (from Wehl, Ibid).

---

[54] Hornsmann, *Ibid*, p.62.

[55] Drower, *Ibid*, pp.36-37.

[56] Hornsmann, *Ibid*, p.73. Hornsmann did not mention the exact dates.

The start and rise of tourism

In 1826 the islander Jacob Andresen Siemens (1794-1849) – carpenter and a member of the island council - opened the *Seebad* or "sea-bath", with a first pavilion on Dune Island; some 100 visitors came in that first summer. Most islanders were sceptical but some fifteen years later Heligoland's economy was unthinkable without the bathing guests; for example, in 1838 the number of visitors was already more than 1,000 and from 1840 onwards the numbers exceeded 2,000 a year! Of course, mainland capitalists started operating regular passenger services to Heligoland. For example, in the summer of 1834 two ferries, the *Patriot* and the *Elbe*, both owned by a company in Hamburg, provided regular services between Hamburg and Heligoland; the journey time was about 14 hours.

Disembarking tourists on Dune Island in the 19th century (from Müller, Ibid).

Founder Siemens and his successors ran the *Seebad Helgoland* as a limited company. Profits were huge. For example, in the period 1848-1854 the shareholders received annual dividends of 75% or more (one time even 107%). When in 1872 the island government took over the Seebad, the price for a share was about 6 times its nominal value![57]

---

[57] Hornsman, *Ibid*, p.59. Siemens's final years were not very pleasant. He often had disputes with other people and even went to London for some legal matters. He died of cholera in London im 1849. Siemens is also renowned for having opened one of the prehistoric burial mounds on the *Oberland*; he was perhaps the first to show that al least one of these hills was a grave. Nowadays, there is a Siemen's memorial in the *Nordostland*.

Heligoland became a popular destination for people who could afford the high prices, including painters, academics and authors. Of course, many pamphlets, tourist guides, paintings and drawings of Heligoland date from this period. Most visitors came from nearby Germany and not from Heligoland's parent country, Great Britain.

One man should be mentioned explicitly, namely doctor Heinrich von Aschen – of Dutch descent - who was the island's bath doctor from 1833 to 1876. Von Aschen wrote books and articles about the healthy effects of a stay on Heligoland. During the winter months von Aschen not only worked in mainland clinics but also made contacts with princes, noblemen, academics and artists, always promoting the *Seebad Helgoland*.

Bathing fashion around 1880 (from Kurt Grobecker, Helgoland, Bildreportagen, *1979).*

As early as 1836, strong regulations for bathing on Dune Island were announced and most of those regulations lasted for many decades. To modern standards, the strangest regulation was the strict separation of a ladies' beach and a gentlemen's beach during bathing hours. Once an official placard read: *'Boys over five years of age are not allowed on the ladies' beach!'* One day, some funny person wrote on the same placard: *'Female types over fifty are not wanted on the men's beach!'*[58]

---

[58] Rickmers, *Ibid*, p.34.

Among the visitors of Heligoland were two famous German poets: Heinrich Heine (1797-1856) and August Heinrich Hoffman von Fallersleben (1798-1874). Heine made his visits around 1830 and Fallersleben did so around 1840. Both poets were politically active, resulting in frequent problems with the authorities in their German home-states[59] but on British Heligoland they could relax! On 26 August 1841, during a stay on Heligoland, Fallersleben wrote the *Lied der Deutschen* (Song of the Germans). Some decades later this song became the German national anthem, well known by the first line of its first stanza, *Deutschland über Alles* (Germany over all). By the way, the actual German anthem only uses the third stanza, starting with *Einigkeit und Recht und Freiheit* (Unity and right and freedom). Nowadays, there is a statue of Fallersleben on the main pier of the main island.

Another visitor became famous in a rather sad way. On 23 August 1853 the 26-year old actress Malwine Erck was struck by lightning on Dune Island, shortly after she had left Saint Peterburg to escape cholera. Her grave in the churchyard on the *Oberland* was a tourist attraction for many decades, partly because of the text on the gravestone: *Hier ruht, vom gold'nen Menschheitsbaume / Verweht durch einen Wetterschlag / Still eine Knosp' im Blütentraume / Zur Reife für den jüngsten Tag*. Freely translated into English: Here rests, from the Golden Tree of Humanity / Struck by Lightning / Only a Bud in Flower's Dream / For Maturing for the Youngest Day.

Grave of the actress Malwine Erck (1827-1853) (from Müller, Ibid).

---

[59] Germany did not yet exist as a national state.

Military events, 1815-1890

After the Napoleonic wars, the British authorities did not use Heligoland as a military base. In 1820 and 1821 the last troops were brought back to Britain. However, in subsequent years the following military events occurred within view of Heligoland:

- On 4 June 1849 there was a sea battle between Denmark and the *German Bund*[60] under the later Admiral Brommy. The Danes retreated into the British waters around Heligoland and so the battle stopped. The Danes were allowed to keep a coal storage on the island and to embark Heligoland pilots[61]. Obviously, the British Governor John Hindmarsh did not execute a strict neutrality policy.

- Between 1854 and 1857, during the Crimean War, the peaceful life of islanders and visitors was disturbed when Heligoland was used as a transfer point for soldiers from mainland Europe on route to the front. Part of the potato fields on the *Oberland* could not be used for some years, because of temporary barracks and military exercises.

- On 9 May 1864 many islanders watched a spectacular sea battle of Danish ships against Prussian and Austrian ones. The battle was not decisive but the Danes were expelled from the German Bight for the rest of the war.

- In 1870, during the French-Prussian War, many French warships cruised within view of Heligoland and pirated a few German merchant vessels[62]. Governor Henry Maxse had been given very strict orders to keep neutrality. And so, the French heard "no" when they tried to purchase coal and water. However, the French used the anchoring grounds east of Dune Island and they profited from the light of the island lighthouse.

---

[60] Germany did not yet exist as a national state.

[61] Rickmers, *Ibid*, p.37.

[62] Rickmers, *Ibid*, p.38. According to George Dower, *Ibid*, p.48 the islanders were furious because they could not use this opportunity to sell to the French navy.

A visitor story of 1845

Heinrich Lambrecht (1812-1898), a German military officer and amateur writer from Oldenburg, visited Heligoland in 1845. He wrote that the prices of wine and food on board his ferry, the *Koning Willem*, were tremendously high[63]:

> Complaints of the passengers were very common but had no effect. In contrast, on the way back another teasing was added, when the waiters accepted the shillings from Hamburg and Holstein - which the passengers took with them from Heligoland - for only one *Groten Bremisch*, although they would even have made profit if they had accepted them for one-and-a-half *Groten Bremisch* (...)

Heinrich Lambrecht and his friends went to a local ball:

> That night there were balls in both the Conversation Hall and in an inn on the *Oberland* called *Grünes Wasser*, which is mainly visited by seamen and island girls. Only a very few island girls visit the Conversation Hall. So, below the well known, unimaginative awful formalities: hat in hand, white gloves, boots, tail costume, all of which we were, being holiday makers, not prepared for; above the happy seamen and red-skirted Heligoland girls with their blinking eyes, rosy cheeks and slender figures. Our choice wasn't difficult and most of us went to the *Oberland* and none of us has probably ever regretted it. At the entrance of the hall we had to pay four shillings for a card, including a glass of wine, grog or punch at the buffet. There were benches along the sides of the room, with lovely dance-willing Heligoland girls. From the front side, a Heligoland girl is very similar to an Oldenburg girl, i.e. she seems to wear a dress similar to our girls. However, when the Heligoland girl turns around, one sees the scarlet skirt with a broad yellow band at the bottom, a very lovely look indeed. (...) Soon we were in the dancing row as well and we tried to entertain our beautiful dancing partners, in the sweat of our faces. We had heard rumours about the virtuousness of the Heligoland girls and those rumours turned out to be quite right.

---

[63] Translated form *Die Lustfahrt nach Helgoland*, various sections from pp.37-51.

From top to bottom: South Beach on the Unterland, *the Conversation Hall and the main island seen from Dune Island (from Wehl,* Ibid*).*

From a tourist guide of 1856

The German draftsman and author Karl Reinhardt (1818-1877) wrote a tourist guide about Heligoland in 1856. Here are a few entries[64]:

At the end of the *Bindfadenallee* we find the island-bath, used by patients who can not cross over to Dune Island, because they get seasick from the slightest movements of the boat. The island-bath is uncomfortable because the bottom is rocky and goes down suddenly. There is no surf, whereas the surf of Dune Island is the main advantage of the sea-bath. Moreover, the water is red and often covered with marine vegetation. As the bath is mainly used by women, a Heligoland man is on the watch each morning and tries to hinder walkers to visit the cliff.

Across the Conversation Hall the street changes into the staircase, where we find some shops selling fruits and other natural products. The landlubbers often purchase mussels from East India and fool their friends at home that they found them on Dune Island. Here you can also rent shotguns - four shillings a day – and purchase powder and bullets. Who likes duelling can find here pistols with the friendly characteristic of hitting the persons standing on the side. Understandably, seconds are strongly recommended either to dig oneself into the sand or to stand *in front of* the duelling persons. (....)

(…) The youth of the island often gathers in front of the Pavilion, hoping to make money by serving the visitors. (…) Some hold a bird in their hands and let it fly for a small fee. They usually appeal to the women, because they release the small animal earlier than the heartless men. Also the trade in sea urchins is in the hands of the young, who catch these animals at low tide behind the cliffs and trade them, either cooked or raw, with or without spines, usually for one or two shillings a piece. (…)

(…) Behind *Möhrmers Gatt* [a cave – A.R.] is a long row of cliffs with small holes and grottos. Who finds the accommodations in town too expensive, can make his Robinsonade here. Fortunately, the Heligoland people are kind enough not to charge anything. Not far from *Möhrmers Gatt* we also find an echo that is often used by the bathing visitors.

---

[64] Translated form *Die Lustfahrt nach Helgoland*, various sections from pp.11-37.

The "strong" governor Maxse (1863-1881) and his successor O'Brien (1881-1888)

In 1863 an energetic man, aged 30 or 31, became governor: Sir Henry Fitzhardinge Berkely Maxse (1832-1883, governor of Heligoland 1863-1881). A few turbulent years followed, partly caused by the strong personality of Maxse, partly by Whitehall (the British Government) and partly by the conservatism of the islanders – including the island council, the *Vorsteherrschaft* - who opposed to any introduction of taxation. In 1864 Whitehall introduced a tax on gambling in order to reduce the huge national debt of the island (about £ 7,000). The islanders protested and Maxse took the side of the islanders. However, Maxse also wanted a constitutional reform, with more power for himself. Moreover, Maxse knew that the introduction of taxation was necessary in order to keep the tourists coming: extra money was needed for the maintenance of the streets, the quays and the ferries to Dune Island. And the island-treasury, mainly managed by the island council, was empty indeed.

In 1864 a new and extremely complex constitution was introduced. This constitution was a mixture of the traditional island government and typical British colonial institutions, with various councils, that were partly elected in the traditional way and partly appointed by the Crown (read: Governor).

In June 1867, thanks to the active policy of Governor Maxse, the Minister for the Colonies, the Duke of Buckingham, stayed a short time on the island. Maxse tried to convince the minister that the island needed a harbour but Maxse did not succeed.

In 1868 a new Constitution was established, making the governor the virtual dictator of the island. The governor was assisted by two councils, one for finance and one for other matters but the members of both councils were appointed by the governor himself. Not very surprisingly, in the same year - 1868 - six British Coast Guards were established, for both life saving and collecting taxes and import duties[65]. The islanders

---

[65] In later years, many young islanders would start a career at the Coastguards.

lost part of their former oligarchy but they generally respected the new law and order.

During his many years of governing (1863-1881), Maxse improved the educational system and introduced compulsory school attendance for children between six and fourteen. Maxse and his wife – Auguste Rudloff, an actress from the Vienna *Hofburg* - strongly lobbied for the island, resulting in many investments, such as a swimming pool and a theatre. William George Black, in *Heligoland and the Islands of the North Sea* (1888), wrote in the highest terms about Maxse[66] and his successor:

> It says much both for Sir Henry Maxse and for the present governor, Sir Terence O'Brien, that this arbitrary government has worked well. To Sir Terence O'Brien particular credit is due. When he came to the island six years ago, it was deeply in debt; it is now free of debt. The streets have been laid with concrete; a new pier built; artesian wells sunk; a steam-lift erected, which does away with the necessity of hauling heavy weights up the Treppe; the Treppe has been in great part rebuilt; (….)
>
> (…) Heligoland is a free port: the only duties levied are on petroleum and spirits. Internally, the boats are taxed, and houses. Bathing guests pay a *kur* tax of four marks each week or less; a family of not more than three persons pays for the same period seven marks; a family of four or more persons pays nine marks. Persons who stay less than three days, or remain after five weeks, pay no tax. Practising physicians, with or without their families, pay no *kur* tax, and receive tickets for free bathing – and bathing is no inconsiderable item in a week's expenses in Heligoland.

When Black's book was published (1888) nobody could know that two years later the British sovereignty over Heligoland would be handed over to Germany, as a result of a diplomatic game in which neither the Heligoland people nor the last British governor (Arthur Barkley, 1888-1890) would play any role.

---

[66] Governor Maxse seems to have had various girl friends on the island (Hornsmann, *Ibid*, p.79). For example, he fathered and acknowledged an extramarital son on the island: Franz Schensky (1871-1957), who would later become the famous island photographer. Today, there is a street named after Governor Maxse on the *Oberland*.

Island man and island woman in the second half of the 19th century (from Müller, Ibid).

1882: on the "Falm" (promenade in the south of the Oberland) with Dune Island in the background (from Müller, Ibid).

83

The German-British Treaty of 1890: Heligoland becomes German

During the 19th century many German diplomats, politicians and military were jealously looking at the tiny British rock only a few dozens of kilometres from the German shore. For example, in 1872 Prince Wilhelm – who would become Kaiser Wilhelm II in 1888 – visited Heligoland and concluded that the island should become German. In 1890 Wilhelm's wish would become reality.

The German-British treaty that resulted in the German ownership of Heligoland was prepared during only a few months in spring and summer of 1890. On 20 March of that year Count Leo van Caprivi became the new Chancellor of Germany, as the successor of the renowned Otto von Bismarck. With the consent of his Kaiser, Caprivi tried to improve the relations with Great Britain. The two powers had somewhat conflicting interests in Africa but were willing to reach some settlement.

In popular writings, it is often said that Heligoland was swapped for the many times larger island of Zanzibar. In reality, the terms of the Treaty were far more complicated. For example, Zanzibar was still "independent" at the time and Germany recognised the British claim for that island. In general one can say that Germany gave up some of its colonial aspirations – not only Zanzibar – in exchange for Heligoland[67].

The German-British treaty contained the following statements regarding the inhabitants of Heligoland:

- Subject to the assent of the British Parliament, the sovereignty over the Island of Heligoland, together with its dependencies, is ceded by Her Britannic Majesty to His Majesty the Emperor of Germany.

---

[67] For an extremely detailed description of the treaty and the corresponding colonial policies in Africa, read the first chapters of the book of Dower, *Ibid*. Dower also made a thorough investigation of the negotiations inside the British government. Queen Victoria opposed, especially because of the rights of the islanders. It is possible that without her intervention the island had been handed over with worse conditions for the islanders.

- The German Government will allow to all persons natives of the territory thus ceded the right of opting for British nationality by means of a declaration to be made by themselves, and [or] in the case of children under the age of consent by their parents or guardians, which must be sent in before 1st January 1892.

- All persons natives of the territory thus ceded and their children born before the date of the signature of the present Agreement are free from the obligation of service in the military and naval forces of Germany.

- Native laws and customs now existing will, as far as possible, remain undisturbed.

- The German Government binds itself not to increase the customs tariff at present in force in the territory thus ceded until 1st January 1910.

- All property rights which private persons or existing corporations have acquired in Heligoland in connections with the British Government are maintained; obligations resulting from them are transferred to His Majesty the Emperor of Germany. It is understood that the above term 'property rights' include the right of signalling now enjoyed by Lloyd's.

- The rights of British fishermen with regard to anchorage in all weathers, to taking in provisions and water, to making repairs, to transhipment of goods, to the sale of fish, and to the landing and drying of nets, remain undisturbed.

Of course, there were German commentators stating that Germany had paid too much for Heligoland, whereas some British commentators stated the opposite. We can be sure that Heligoland might have remained British if more powerful British politicians had foreseen the German military plans with the islands – and the German plans for a huge *Kriegsmarine* (German Navy) challenging the Royal Navy. Some wise people had already warned for German militarisation of the island before the handover, for example W.G. Black in his book *Heligoland and the Islands of the North Sea* (1888) and the renowned island naturalist and official government interpreter, Heinrich Gätke[68].

---

[68] Heinrich Gätke (1814-1897), born and raised on the German mainland, was a painter, businessman and naturalist. He came to Heligoland in 1837 and married an island woman in 1841.

In the morning of 9 August 1890 – the last day of British sovereignty - British soldiers were still busy removing the few British military installations – some of which dated from the 18th century - on Heligoland. On the afternoon of that day Governor Arthur Barkley officially handed over the island to the German minister Von Boetticher.

Sea urchins for sale! (from Müller, Ibid)

During many years he was the official government interpreter. Tourists knew him for his beautiful collections of paintings and stuffed birds. Gätke's book *Die Vogelwarte Helgoland* (reprinted in 1987) is still a classic. There is an English edition of 1895, *Heligoland as an Ornithological Observatory*.

A visit of a German upper class girl in 1893

In 1893 a German upper-class girl, aged about 16, visited Heligoland. Her diary was published in the book *Helgoland, das Reise- und Lesebuch für die Insel* (2002). Here are a few entertaining entries:

(Sunday, 23 July 1893)

How fantastic! I may travel to Heligoland with my friend Gertrud and her parents! Two weeks on a small island in the middle of the North Sea but also in the middle of a stylish world, so exciting, so romantic! My mother and I will order my travelling clothes at the women's dressmaker tomorrow already. Of course I also need a bathing costume, although Gertrud told me you could simply dive naked into the water behind the bathing-cars. But I will never contemplate about doing so! I don't understand the style of bathing with the bathing-cars anyway.

(Monday, 24 July 1893)

The new clothes have been ordered. I will get three summer dresses at ankle-length, a proper bathing costume and two fantastic evening gowns from silk and taffeta showing my waist perfectly. But I am most excited by the white tennis dress, a gift from my aunt. Upon my objection that I could not play tennis at all, my cousin Richard immediately offered me some lessons. And so, we had some tiresome hours on the tennis fields. (....)

The day of travel to the island was Friday, 4 August 1893:

(...) The ship was bobbing on the waves ever more. We enjoyed each up and down! Finally we decided to sit down on a deck chair. When we had just sat down, we heard a voice behind us, saying: "Hello, the ladies seem to be in good humour." We turned around and so we met a very friendly young man. His name was Wilhelm Hansen and it was his third trip to Heligoland already. He seemed to be thrilled to get to know us, and so he immediately started telling us a lot about the island. I will write about that tomorrow; just now, I am too exhausted to write any further.

(Saturday, 5 August 1893)

I had a long lie-in and was strengthened by a hearty English breakfast. After all, the island belonged to England until most recently. In 1890 it became German in exchange for Sansibar. Yesterday, on the ship, Wilhelm – by the way, he looks very fantastic – told me all this (....)

(Monday, 6 August 1893)

The church bells awakened us and we went to Dune Island very early, because bathing time is only between 7 a.m. and 1 p.m. To begin with, you pay a little fee for the transfer. A typical characteristic of this island is that absolutely nothing is free of charge. (....)

Our group came on land and our group was split up; the men went to the men's bath and the women to the women's bath. (...)

(...) Everyone chose a bathing-car and gave a mark to the bath servant with his impressive figure. Then we went in. I was astonished by the space and there was even a small mirror! I started changing clothes immediately and when I was almost naked I heard a knocking. I stiffened. Did somebody try to get in just now? But suddenly the car started moving and I was almost thrown out of the door. At the last moment, I managed to hold a bar. Aha, the knocking had only been the sign for entering the water! I thought nothing could happen to me any more and pulled on my bathing suit. I opened the door and planned to walk down the steps into the sea, until I saw a number of completely naked female types. They seemed to be not shy at all but I was so astonished that I missed one step and fell with my front into the cold water! (....)

(...) Fortunately, the rest of the day went quiet. We walked to Reimer's Pavilion and went back at 2 p.m. with the last boat, strengthened and in an excellent mood. After a lengthy afternoon break in our chambers we went into the *Kurleben*: coffee and cake in the music pavilion, then dinner in the Conversation Hall where a chapel later started playing dancing music. My *Kavalier* impressed with excellent dancing and so I really had to fight a self-contest in order to allow other young men on my dancing card as well.

On 9 August 1893 the Kaiser visited the island. The girl wrote that day numerous islanders and visitors greeted the Kaiser, who, as always, showed a great interest in the island's military installations.

The gentlemen's beach on Dune Island in the 19th century.

The ladies' beach on Dune Island in the 19th century.

After bathing (all pictures on this page from Müller, Ibid).

89

CHAPTER 9. Heligoland is German (since 1890)

1890-1914: *Heligoland is militarised*

On 10 August 1890 the handover of Heligoland to Germany was celebrated in a huge ceremony; some 11,000 guests, including Kaiser Wilhelm II, were on the island. In the spring of 1891, Heligoland became an official community inside the Kingdom of Prussia. The official spelling for the island soon became "Helgoland" instead of "Heligoland".

During the subsequent years, many new buildings were modernised or erected: modernisation of the *Kurhaus* (Cure House, the former Conversation Hall) (1893), a new swimming pool with hot water (1895), the North Sea Museum (1897), the Aquarium (1902), a new lighthouse (1902) and a new elevator to the *Oberland* (1903)[69].

The Prussian lighthouse and its lower British predecessor aroud 1902, shortly before the latter was demolished (impression of Anneke de Vries from a contemporary photo (Picture 377 of the CD Alt Helgoland in 2260 Bildern).

---

[69] Kuckuck, *Ibid*, p.117.

The main island became a complete military fortress. During the early 1890s German military engineers installed massive guns on the *Oberland* and built a tunnel between the *Unterland* and *Oberland*. As a result, the islanders lost farming fields on the *Oberland* and farming entirely ceased around 1910. Of course, the island had to house hundreds of soldiers and construction workers, causing important - and generally not very pleasant - changes in the daily life of the islanders.

Heavy guns on the Oberland *during the Kaiser period. In the background we see the Prussian lighthouse and a signal tower (impression of Anneke de Vries from a contemporary photo (Picture 451 of the CD* Alt Helgoland in 2260 Bildern*))*.

In 1906 military engineers started the construction of South Harbour, depriving the islanders of some of their important fishing grounds, including good spots for lobster. Moreover, South Beach (in the *Unterland*) could no longer be used to pull boats on land in case of stormy weather. When South Harbour was completed, the Heligoland boatmen were not allowed to use it, because it was an exclusively military harbour.

Kaiser Wilhelm II was very proud of his new territory and military base; he visited Heligoland more than twenty times between 1890 and 1914, often with his huge private yacht *Hohenzollern*. On one occasion, the Kaiser met an island diver in the harbour, leading to an entertaining discussion. The Kaiser started with[70]: *"Do you have a lot of work here?"* Diver: *"Yes, I've a lot of work."* Kaiser: *"Then you make a lot of money."* Diver:

---

[70] Rickmers, *Ibid*, p.49.

"Yes, that's right." Kaiser: *"Then you've definitely more money than I!"* Diver: *"But Majesty, you're not a diver."*

Prior to 1900, the Heligoland treasury got revenue from the so-called *Fremdentrauungen*, i.e. the weddings between non-islanders on the island – weddings that were very popular among members of the upper classes. When in 1900 the Prussian marriage legislation was introduced on Heligoland, the overseas wedding practices had to stop. Prussia paid compensation to Heligoland for ten years.

1 January 1910 was an important day for something that did *not* happen. On that date – mentioned in the treaty with Britain of 1890 - the Prussian government could have used the opportunity to integrate Heligoland into the Prussian tax legislation. However, the Prussian government did not do so and Heligoland has kept its tax-free status until the present day. Ironically, during the Kaiser period the Kingdom of Prussia[71] even had to pay compensation to the German Empire for the missed import duties caused by the status of Heligoland![72]

Around 1910 the islanders had to share their tiny island with many soldiers. The islanders had lost their former quiet life but when war broke out in September 1914, they even lost their island.

1914-1918: First World War, population in exile on the mainland

On 2 and 3 September 1914, shortly after the beginning of the First World War, all 3,427 islanders were forced to leave their island, with hand luggage only. Their houses would be used by some 4,000 German military for the next four years. The island people were dispersed over many places in northern Germany. However, the lifeboat crew stayed on the island and carried out some brave rescue operations[73]. During the war

---

[71] Wilhem II was both King of Prussia and Kaiser of the German Empire.

[72] *Helgoland, das Reise- und Lesebuch für die Insel*, 2002, pp.80-81.

[73] Kuckuck, *Ibid*, p.124.

only a few islanders were allowed to return to the island, such as the photographer, the keeper of the bookshop and some eighty fishermen[74].

The war in the North Sea was strongly influenced by the German base on Heligoland, from where many German submarines started their voyages. Remarkably enough, the heavy guns on the *Oberland* - twenty-four guns with diameters between 15 and 30 centimetres - never interfered in any battle, because those battles occurred either too far from the island or during hazy weather. However, the heavy guns were so deterrent that the Allies rarely approached the island and never attempted to conquer it; Allied plans to invade the island were never executed[75]. If Heligoland had not existed, the Allied fleets would have come – and would have laid minefields – much closer to Germany's mainland shores.

Heavy gun on the Oberland, *Kaiser period (impression of Anneke de Vries from a contemporary photo (Picture 390 of the CD* Alt Helgoland in 2260 Bildern*))*.

---

[74] Rickmers, *Ibid*, p.60.

[75] For many details, see Dower, *Ibid*, pp.153-182. One of the British plan-makers was Winston Churchill.

1918-1933: Heligoland in the Weimar Republic

Germany lost the war in November 1918. As a result, in the winter of 1918/19 most islanders returned to their houses – which had often been neglected or plundered. Some islanders tried to persuade British authorities that Britain should re-annex the island[76].

According to the peace treaty, Heligoland's military installations had to be dismantled. For that purpose, many Allied officials were on the island between February 1920 and June 1922. Contacts between islanders and the Allied officials were very good; for example, many officials wore Heligoland clothes when they were off duty! However, the Allied Commission did not do the demolition very thoroughly; and so, less than 15 years later the Nazi regime could easily re-use parts of the old works, such as the tunnel connecting the *Oberland* with the southern harbour. On the other hand, some important dams, protecting the vulnerable island from heavy seas, had been weakened or even destructed; even the lifeboat station was at risk[77].

After they had come home in 1918/19, the islanders quickly returned to their traditional economic activities as fishing and tourism; fortunately, they could now use South Harbour, something that had been impossible prior to 1914. New visitor attractions were built: a tennis court, a swimming pool and a football pitch. In 1926 the first commercial flight - by seaplane - to Heligoland, from Cuxhaven, was carried out.

In 1919 the number of visitors stood at 11,000 but that number jumped to more than 180,000 in 1929! In subsequent years the number of visitors went down as a result of the Great Depression. After 1933 the numbers rose again – but by that time the Nazis had taken over the island, as will be described in the next paragraph.

---

[76] For details, see Dower, *Ibid*, pp.184-185.
[77] Dower, *Ibid*, p.190.

1933-1939: the first years of the Nazis

On 14 January 1933 there were free elections for Heligoland's community council and the Nazi Party – the NSDAP – got three out of nine seats. A few weeks later, the Nazis would come to power, meaning the end of democracy in Germany, including Heligoland. Later during that year two elected members of the island's community council - August Kuchlenz and Erich Friedrichs - were even sent to a concentration camp because of their opposition to Nazism; they were released after they had signed a paper stating that they would not tell about their life inside the concentration camp[78].

In the early years of the Nazi regime the number of visitors to the island went up again. In those days, Nazi organisations as *Kraft durch Freude* (literally "Strength through Joy") organised short and cheap holidays for working class people, including one-day trips to Heligoland in summer! In 1936 the official number of visitors was over 240,000, many of whom were wearing or carrying Nazi-symbols. The nature of this mass-tourism was, of course, very different from the upper-class tourism of the 19th century.

Evidently, the Nazis started remilitarising the island soon after they had come to power. Within a few years, some areas were for military only, notably South Harbour and the *Oberland* outside the village and the narrow coastal footpath[79]. Some Nazi-VIPS, including Adolf Hitler himself, made visits to the island and inspected the new military installations. In the late 1930s the present *Nordostland* and most of present Dune Island, with its landing strip, were formed with sand from the surrounding sea-bottom. In fact, these extensions were only the beginning of the project called *Hummerschere*, literally Lobster Claws. Both islands had to be extended and shaped like lobster claws. Inside the various dams, one of the largest military ice-free ports would be created. The project was never completed, partly because of the German military successes in early 1940, after which the Nazis could use many other ice-free harbours, from northern Norway to south-western France!

---

[78] Krüss, *Ibid*, 2005, p.31.

[79] R.M.Lockley, *I Know an Island, 1938*, p.167. Lockley described the situation in October 1936.

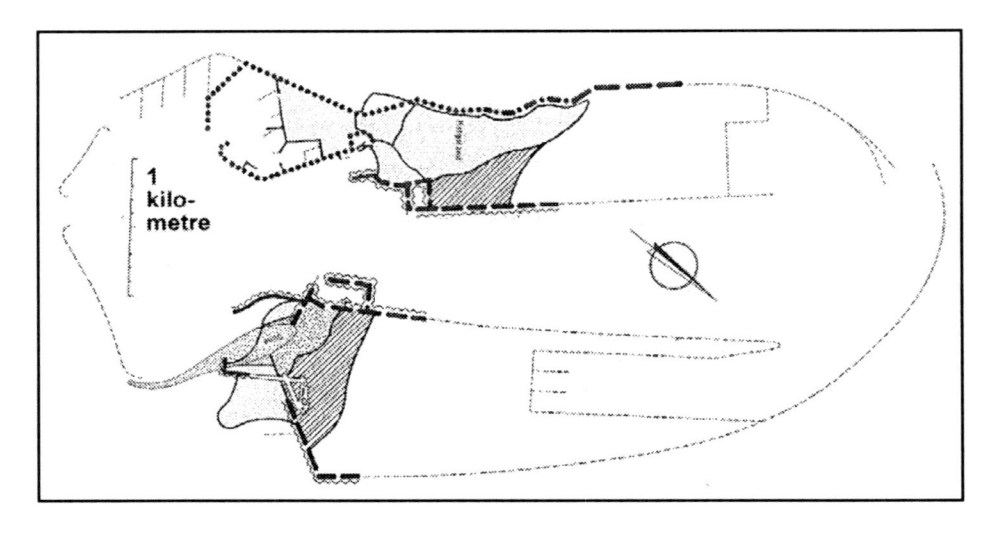

Project Hummerschere. *The dotted lines show never realised plans. The entire German Navy could be housed in this ice-free harbour (from* Die Kueste, *1990)!*

Of course, the Nazis manifested themselves on the island in many ways[80]. For example, in August 1935 *Reichstag* (Parliament) member Heinrich wrote in the Nazi periodical *Stürmer* that the Heligolanders still had to be taught anti-Semitism. A Heligoland tourist pamphlet of 1938 stated that the new *Kurhaus* (Cure House) had been made of "northern brick" and that "Jews are by no means wanted, for Heligoland is a German herald and wishes to be so" (*Juden sind allerdings unerwünscht, denn Helgoland ist ein deutscher Vorposten und will das sein*).

In 1939 a Jewish woman, living on Heligoland, lost her "Arian" husband and went with her children to Hamburg. In 1944 the woman and one daughter were sent to a concentration camp; both survived the war. Some islanders supported Nazism themselves but others did not and had to be careful not to be charged with something. For example, in 1938/39 some men from Heligoland and Cuxhaven were charged with homosexuality, leading to some suicides and executions. In 1943 a barber was betrayed for some "thought crime". He was arrested by the Gestapo and executed one year later.

---

[80] Sources for the following sections: *Hegoland, das Reise- und Lesebuch für die Insel*, 2002, p.101-2 and Herms, *Ibid*, pp.84-5

A British visitor in 1936

Ronald Mathias Lockley (1903-2000), a Welshman and later a New Zealander, was a naturalist, island traveller and author. He visited Heligoland in October 1936 and had his diary printed in one chapter of his book *I know an Island* (1938). Lockley wrote about the *Fanggarten*, as well as bird hunting by the islanders. A few entries:

(21 October 1936)

Woodcock[81] were everywhere on the island, and so were the gunners, who got 350 of them, one man bagging sixty. Both these figures, Drost [from the *Fanggarten* – A.R.] says, are records within living memory. These birds are sold for two shillings each, and exported to Hamburg.

Living on Heligoland is quite inexpensive. I pay 2.50 marks (26 marks to the pound) for bed and breakfast. Dinner – one mark, gratuity refused, at a "Mittagstisch" – a communal eating-house popular with all grades, where you sit round a huge table and have as much hot soup as you care to take from a large silver tureen. This is followed by meat and vegetables, and a sweet. No drinks are served, not even water. Supper I buy on my way home – rolls, butter, cake, jam, and tea – about 0.30 marks. Altogether not four marks, or four shillings a day.

Out of curiosity I entered the one cinema (best seats, 1.50 marks – military half-price), and enjoyed an excellent nature film and a light drama.

My lodgings are comfortable. Electricity brightens the little houses here. Water has to be imported if the amount collected in underground tanks from the wooden eaves-gutters runs low. Heligoland rainwater is said to be of a very good flavour because of the earthenware tiles and the wooden gutters, but I was also told that it often tastes gamy; this is due to the great number of small birds that drop exhausted down the pipes leading to the tanks on a night of heavy migration. (….)

(24 October 1936)

Went out with the young fisherman who was to shoot sea-birds for food. His was a typical Heligoland-boat, more bluff in the bow than the

---

[81] *Scolopax rusticola*, German *Waldschnepfe*.

bluffest English canal barge, seventeen feet long, with 4-h.p. engine and square-stemmed Scandinavian oars.(…)

A razorbill[82] rose near the boat. The fisherman gave me the tiller. As he moved forward to the bow he shot the bird.

He crouched low on sighting the next victim – a kittiwake[83]. It swerved away, but he brought it questing to us with a very successful imitation of the cry of the Arctic tern[84], "Ss!" and its peculiar whistle. Then he hurled the dead razorbill far out in the air. The kittiwake hovered over us, curious and alert at this suggestion of another bird diving for food. In this manner he decoyed and shot about eight more kittiwakes, a guillemot[85], two young Arctic terns, and two mature little gulls[86], the first I have ever seen alive. A dead fulmar-petrel[87] we chanced upon was thenceforth used as a bait to throw in the air. Shots did not seem to disturb the birds in the least; they were more interested in the bodies of their companions in the water. There were oil patches on most birds.

But my companion thought little of his bag, which filled half a large fish basket. It was possible to shoot 200 kittiwakes in a day. His father held a record with 286. (…)

Finally, here are some entries from Lockley's diary referring to the Nazi regime. A German journalist of the time writing this way would have got problems with the Nazi censorship – or worse!

(Sunday, 25 October 1936)

A quiet day writing notes and catching a few birds in the garden. High wind and rain continuing. Not many people go to church. There is a dance-hall. At the cinema, where films are changed weekly, saw t-day a very poor show: a dull, stale news-reel, and two or three films frankly propagating the Nazi cause – road-making scenes, marching, counter-marching, goose-stepping, and fierce speeches. Yet nearly four hundred people or about an eighth of the population filled the building, so that most of the folk must see the films in a seven-day week.

---

[82] *Alca torda*, German *Tordalk*.

[83] *Rissa tridactyla*, German *Driezehnmöwe*.

[84] *Sterna paradisae*, German *Küstenseeschwalbe*.

[85] *Uria aalge*, German *Trottellumme*.

[86] *Larus minutus*, German *Zwergmöwe*.

[87] *Fulmaris glacialis*, German *Eissturmvogel*.

> Yesterday there had been a demonstration by some political organization – I did not know what – at which all young men had to attend. And almost every day a new "thought" appears on the notice-boards on the staircase joining Upper and Lower Towns. I notice that "Bolschevismus" and "Return to our Colonies" seem to be the two most burning themes. All this, and the "Fly your Swastika" and other patriotic law and etiquette, combined with the swarms of the people in the streets, is suggestive of the law, order, and communism of the ant-heap – warriors and workers complete.

Houses on the Oberland before the Second World War (from Kuckuk's Nordseelotse). If all buildings of those days would still exist, the streets of Heligoland might have formed a UNESCO-protected site nowadays!

1939-1945: Second World War

On 1 September 1939, at the beginning of the Second World War, Heligoland was immediately closed to tourists. By the way, the two islands were not attractive to tourists any more, because civilians were not allowed to enter Dune Island, South Harbour and many parts of the *Nordostland* and the *Oberland*. In fact, Heligoland was nothing but bunkers, carbon wire, guns and a military harbour. For transport of heavy things, there was a narrow-gauge railway from South Harbour through a tunnel until far into the *Oberland*.

Remarkably enough, most islanders stayed on the island that was now overcrowded with German military, specialised construction workers from various countries, prisoners of war and forced labourers. On some days the total population must have been around 9,000. Needless to say, many ships were needed to supply the island with food, drinking water, ammunition, and so on.

Soldier's houses on the Oberland, *Nazi period (impression of Anneke de Vries from a contemporary photo (Picture 1275 of the CD* Alt Helgoland in 2260 Bildern*))*.

Both islands were often bombarded by Allied aircraft. In order to protect the population, many hiding places and corridors were constructed inside the sandstone; in the end, the total length of all corridors was some twelve kilometres. Each family and each group of military had its own hiding place inside the sandstone. Needless to say, the shelters for the forced labourers were less convenient; they were even locked up during

Allied attacks at night. The forced labourers knew that the island commander had ordered to kill them all in case of an Allied landing on Heligoland[88].

In fact, the military importance of Heligoland should not be overestimated. In 1943 or 1944 the numbers of military and workers were diminished, because they were more urgently needed elsewhere. For example, island boys of the *Hitlerjugend* replaced some Navy men[89].

In early April 1945 a group of brave islanders, with Erich Friedrichs[90] (*Eäk Funk* in *Halunder*) as their leader, were in contact with the Allies in order to hand over the island without bloodshed by hoisting the white flag. Friedrichs and his men would commit their *coup d'etat* on 18 April 1945, however, on the early morning of that day the Gestapo rounded up the resistance group. Three days later Friedrichs and six comrades were executed by a fire squad in Cuxhaven.

On 18 April 1945, around noon, Heligoland got a mega-bombardment, comparable with the well-known – and earlier - mega-bombardments of Dresden, Hamburg and Berlin. The total attack lasted about two hours and was carried out by more than 1,000 aircraft and about 7,000 bombs. Twelve civilians and 116 military were killed. The island was left uninhabitable. During the successive days, all people on the island were transported to the mainland.

1945-1952: Heligoland is uninhabited

Between 1945 and 1952 most Heligoland people were dispersed over various spots in the British occupation zone in northwestern Germany. The Royal Air Force used both islands as practising grounds for its bombing crews. On 18 April 1947 – the day of the "Big Bang" - British military engineers organised one of the largest non-nuclear detonations

---

[88] Herms, *Ibid*, p.93-94: information from the former Ukrainian prisoner of war A.I.Plachtij.

[89] Herms, *Ibid*, p.96.

[90] The Nazis had already held Friedrichs (1890-1945) in a concentration camp in 1933.

of all times; the results are still visible in the form of the area nowadays called *Mittelland* – formerly the southwest corner of the *Oberland*.

Both British and German authorities – from Schleswig-Holstein - had to make official announcements that landings on the islands were not allowed and even risky. In 1951 persons entering the island were even threatened with punishments up to one year in prison. Nonetheless, some islanders sometimes landed one or both islands. Of course, peaceful demonstrations of islanders[91], often dressed in traditional clothes, occurred frequently in the places of exile.

Some British authorities were willingly enough to give Heligoland back to its people but the RAF wished to keep Heligoland as a practice ground. In February 1952 the RAF threw its last bombs and on 1 March of that year the island was finally given back to the islanders, for which 1 March has been a local holiday ever since.

1952 to present

On 1 March 1952 the island was given back to the islanders. A period of reconstruction started, because there were no buildings to live in any more. Ironically, one of the highest buildings was still standing upright, only slightly damaged: the former anti-aircraft tower! The tower became the new lighthouse and has remained so until the present day.

During the first years, many islanders had to live in houseboats and tourists could only stay in tents on Dune Island. During the 1950s and early 1960s many of the present houses were built; functional but somewhat monotonous. Many houses were built with extra rooms, so that one or more rooms could be rented to tourists. The building of huge hotels was rejected.

---

[91] Including an open letter to the British General Robertson, written in 1949 by island-born James Krüss (1926-1997) who would later become one of Germany's famous authors of children's books. Many books are inspired by Heligoland and are translated into English, e.g. *The Lighthouse on the Lobster Cliffs*.

Sea view of the lighthouse from the west (by Anneke de Vries, from a photo by the author).

During the first years, many islanders had to live in houseboats and tourists could only stay in tents on Dune Island. During the 1950s and early 1960s many of the present houses were built; functional but somewhat monotonous. Many houses were built with extra rooms, so that one or more rooms could be rented to tourists. The building of huge hotels was rejected.

In the beginning most houses had cisterns for collecting rainwater. Since the 1980s those cisterns have generally been used for other purposes because of the construction of an impressive comprehensive power-plant for drinking-water - now mainly derived from seawater – and electricity and heating. Everything is produced in an extremely environmental-friendly way but the prices are much higher than on the German mainland.

Of course, virtually all jobs on the island – except for the few dozens of employees of the *Biologische Anstalt Helgoland*, the biological centre - depend directly or indirectly on mass tourism, including sick people visiting the island in order to go on a cure. Around 1990 the annual number of visitors stood at around 700,000 a year but nowadays the numbers are below 500,000[92]. No doubt, Heligoland has lost attractiveness because of the increasing possibilities of cheap foreign holidays to the south. Indeed, travelling to and staying on Heligoland is not cheap and there are no last minute tickets of one Euro to the island!

In the 1990s Heligoland's tax-free status – or, more exactly, VAT-free and excise-free-status – was under pressure. In 1999 the European Union ordered to discontinue tax-free shopping on ferries and flights inside the EU but Heligoland's status was officially reconfirmed. If Heligoland had lost its tax-free status, many shops with spirits, perfume and cigarettes would have closed and dozens of jobs would have gone lost.

Traditionally, many Heligoland men made money with transporting passengers between the large passenger ships and the landing piers, because those ships could - and can - not enter South Harbour. However, nowadays an increasing number of visitors is travelling on catamaran-vessels docking at the quays in South Harbour. On a modern summer afternoon you see about five traditional ferries lying in the Straits of Heligoland but in the 1970s you saw ten or more.

Evidently, the number of islanders has decreased, from about 2,400 in the mid-1970s to about 1,400 now. No doubt, Heligoland will remain an attraction for many people but nobody can predict the visiting numbers, the employment and the profit margins for the tourist entrepreneurs.

The Wappen von Hamburg *and a* Börtboot *for embarking or disembarking passengers, with Dune Island in the background (by Anneke de Vries, from a photo by the author).*

---

[92] See the Appendix for precise statistics.

APPENDIX: population statistics

All data in this appendix are derived from Erich-Nummel Krüss, *Chronologie der Insel Helgoland*, 2005

	Schleswig-Gottorp time, 1544-1714	
	INHAB.	*OTHER STATISTICS*
1550	c. 300	
1615	300-400	68 island pilots
1640	c. 360	
1672	c. 900	172 Bürlott-owners
1680		42 mariner's widows
		1684-89, island is temporarily Danish
1685		96 pilots
1696	c. 960	93 mariner's widows
	Danish time, 1714-1807	
1723	c. 2,300	
1740	c. 1,900	
1751	c. 2,000	
1790	1,650	Island pilots are piloting about 400 ships into the rivers Elbe, Weser, Eider
1791	1,700	
1802		about 300 island pilots
1807	2,041	

	British time, 1807-1890	
	INHABITANTS	VISITORS
1825	2,211	
1826		100
1829		200
1838		1,030
1841		2,000
1849	2,152	
1851	2,180	2,160
	1854-57, many (perhaps hundreds) of soldiers in barracks on the *Oberland*, as station on route to the Crimean War fronts.	
1858		2,218
1863		3,000
1868		3,412
1871	1,912	
1874		2,350
1875		1,540
1880		4,000
1881	2,001	
1883		5,000
1885		7,360
1887		9,600
1888		8,320

German Empire, 1890-1914		
	INHABITANTS	VISITORS
1890	2,086	12,732
1895	2,152	14,270
1900	2,307	34,400
1905	2,334	48,999
1910		75,400
1913		101,400
World War I, 1914-1918, only military on the islands		

Between the wars, 1918-1939		
	INHABITANTS	VISITORS
1919		11,009
1923		82,623
1927		111,494
1928		162,731
1929		181,315
1930		138,331
1931	2,531	107,478
1932	2,601	105,408
1935		246,200
World War II, 1939-1945, no tourists but up to 8,000 people on Heligoland		
Heligoland is uninhabited, 1945-1952		

Heligoland in the Federal Republic of Germany, 1953 to present

	INHAB.	VISITORS
1953	88	39,100
1954	253	65,200
1955	350	143,500
1956	868	167,438
1957	1,483	230,131
1958	1,196	279,793
1959	1,903	382,658
1960	1,700	382,721
1961	1,852	413,900
1962	2,200	449,344
1963	2,351	490,391
1964	2,809	550,950
1965	2,984	560,013
1966	3,388	570,774
1967	2,705	589,856
1968		625,804
1969	3,328	724,950
1970	2,395	793,005
1971		831,387
1972		796,537
1973		822,276
1974	2,398	719,259
1975	2,396	702,639
1976	2,341	716,107
1977	2,341	676,585
1978	2,313	635,678
1979	2,308	590,292

	INHAB.	VISITORS
1980	2,200	559,916
1981	2,018	567,791
1982	1,978	558,693
1983	2,000	496,467
1984	1,953	468,648
1985	1,958	455,962
1986	1,905	490,801
1987	1,889	462,108
1988	1,804	478,700
1989	1,703	482,093
1990	1,737	593,065
1991	1,740	683,032
1992	1,749	723,927
1993	1,731	668,946
1994	1,737	610,237
1995	1,689	555,653
1996	1,631	505,414
1997	1,651	538,573
1998	1,612	485,432
1999	1,566	542,625
2000	1,570	538,692
2001	1,542	555,904
2002	1,504	559,717
2003	1,488	563,160
2004	1,438	469,716

LITERATURE

English

Black, William Geroge, *Heligoland and the Islands of the North Sea*, William Blackwood and Sons, Edinburgh and London, 1888

Black, William George, "Heligoland – the Island of Green, Red and White", *Blackwood's Edinburgh Magazine*, August 1890, pp.160-171

Black, William George, "From Heligoland to Helgoland", *National Review*, volume 58, 1911, pp.317-322

Drower, George, *Heligoland – The True Story of German Bight and the Island that Britain Betrayed*, Sutton Publishing, Gloucestershire, 2002

Lockley, Ronald Matthias, *I Know an Island*, George G. Harap & Company Limited, London, Toronto, Sydney and Bombay, 1938

Dutch

Sören Sörensen et al, *Vogels van de Noordatlantische eilanden*, GMB Uitgeverij, Haarlem 1993

German

Ahrens, Claus, *Vorgeschichte des Kreises Pinneberg und der Insel Helgoland*, Wachholtz Verlag Neumünster, 1966

Bairlein, Franz, *Institut für Vogelforschung "Vogelwarte Helgoland"*, 1992

Die Lustfahrt nach Helgoland, Verlag und Buchhandlung Maren Knauss, 1987

Die Küste – Archiv für Forschung und Technik an der Nord- und Ostsee, Kuratorium für Forschung im Küsteningenieurwesen, 1990

Fiedler, Walter, *Helgoland*, Breklumer Verlag, Breklum, 1988

Friedrichs, Kurt, *Umkämpftes Helgoland, Der Leidensweg eines Inselvolkes*, Verlag für Helgoland-Literatur, 1988

Gätke, Heinrich, *Die Vogelwarte Helgoland*, Verlag für Helgoland-Literatur, 1987 (reprint from 1900)

Grobecker, Kurt, *Helgoland, Bildreportagen aus dem vergangenen Jahrhundert*, Hoffman und Campe, 1979

Helgoland, das Reise- und Lesebuch für die Insel, Edition Temmen, Bremen, 2002

Herms, Michael, *Flaggenwechsel auf Helgoland – Der Kampf um einen militärischen Vorposten in der Nordsee*, Ch. Links Verlag, Berlin, 2002

Hornsmann, Otto-Erwin, *Geschichte und Geschichten der Insel Helgoland*, Museum Helgoland, 2006

Hubrich-Messow, Gundula, *Sagen und Legenden von der Insel Helgoland*, Husum Druck- und Verlagsgesellscaft mbH u.Co.KG, 2004

Goemann, Olaf, *"Echt" Helgoländer Hummer*, Kohlrenken Verlag Oldenburg, 1990

Krüss, Erich-Nummel, *Fischer-Schiffer-Lotsen*, Museum Helgoland, 2003

Krüss, Erich-Nummel, *Chronologie der Insel Helgoland*, Museum Helgoland, 2005

Kuckuck, Paul, *Der Nordseelootse*, Otto Meissners Verlag, Hamburg, 1924

Müller, W.F., *Helgoland mit Zeichnungen von Rudolph Crell*, Verlag Schuster, Leer, 1977 (reprint from 1882)

OAG Helgoland, *Ornithologischer Jahresbericht Helgoland*, various editions

Rickmers, Henry and Frank Woosman (with co-operation by Beate Griese), *Helgoland – eine Insel auf dem Wege nach Europa*, Niederelbe-Verlag, 1992

Schmidt-Thomé, Paul, *Helgoland – Seine Dünen-Insel, die umgebenden Klippen und Meeresgruende*, Gebrüder Bornträger, Berlin/Stuttgart, 1987

Stühmer, H.H., Späth, C. & Schmid, F., *Fossilien Helgolands* (two volumes), Niederelbe-Druck, Otterndorfer Verlagsdruckerei H. Kuster KG, Otterndorf /Helgoland, 1982

Vahlendieck, August Wilhelm, *Das Witte Kliff von Helgoland*, Nordfriisk Institut, Bredstedt, 1992

Vauk, Gottfried and others, *Geschichte der Vogelwarte Helgoland*, Niederelbe-Druck, Otterndorfer Verlagsdruckerei H. Kuster KG, Otterndorf, 1977

Wallmann, Elisabeth, *Die Zerstörung Helgolands durch die Bombardierung am 18. April 1945*, Evang.-luth. Kirchengemeinde Helgoland, 1995

Wehl, Feodor, *Ganz Helgoland, Illustrierter Fremdenführer van Hamburg nach Helgoland und Begleiter auf der Insel in allen ihren Theilen*, Verlag für Helgoland-Literatur, 1996 (reprint from 1861)

Websites about Heligoland

www.helgoland.de

http://www.museum-helgoland.de/

http://www.awi-bremerhaven.de/BAH/aquarium.html

http://www.fh-oow.de/cms/ifv/index.php?action=sprache&lang=de

Website of the author:

www.aworldofislands.com

Website of the artist:

www.annekedevries.nl

Printed in the United Kingdom
by Lightning Source UK Ltd.
136056UK00001B/395/A